· NO ·. PHOTOGRAPHING

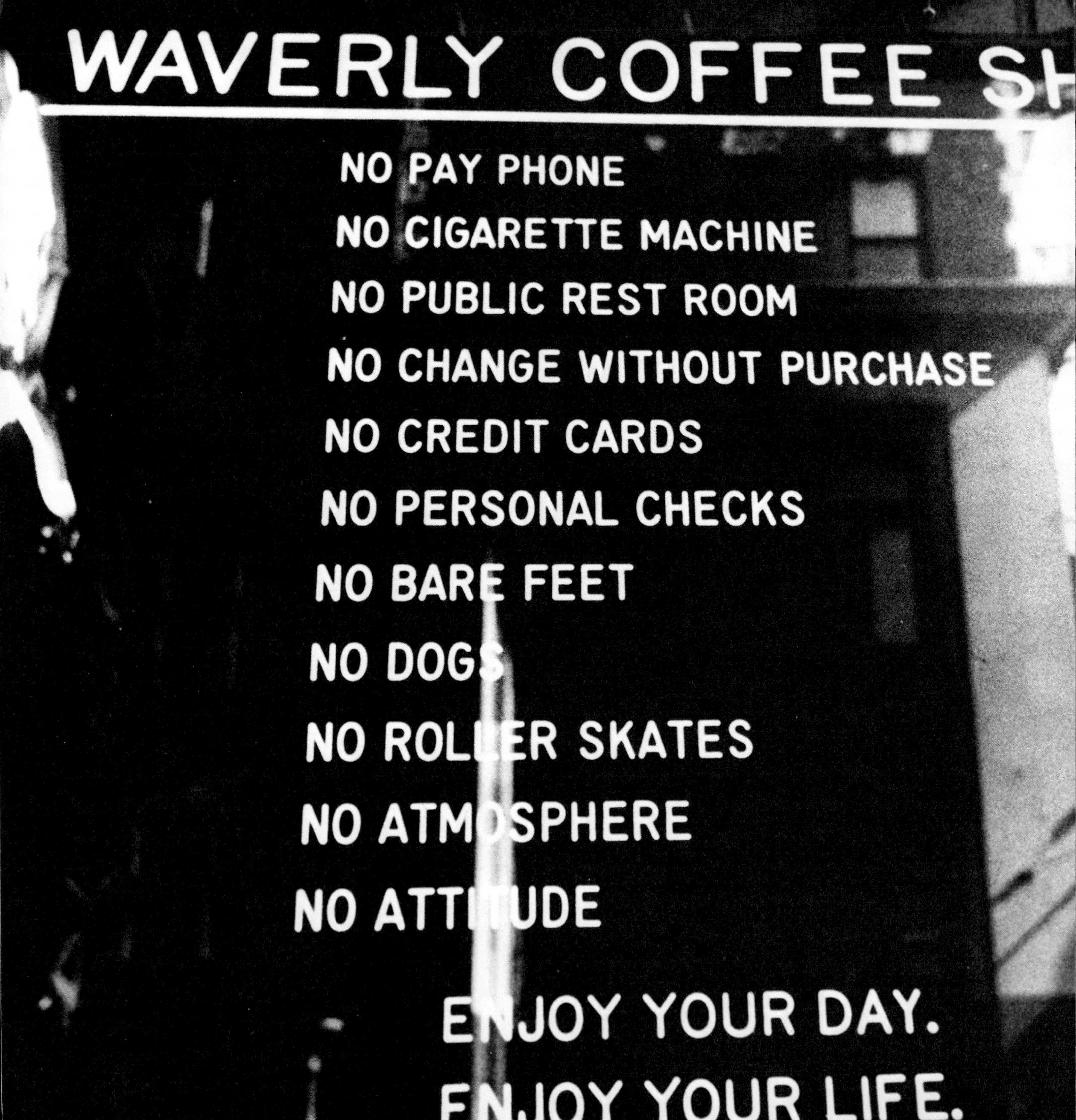

WAVERLY COFFEE SH

NO PAY PHONE
NO CIGARETTE MACHINE
NO PUBLIC REST ROOM
NO CHANGE WITHOUT PURCHASE
NO CREDIT CARDS
NO PERSONAL CHECKS
NO BARE FEET
NO DOGS
NO ROLLER SKATES
NO ATMOSPHERE
NO ATTITUDE

ENJOY YOUR DAY.
ENJOY YOUR LIFE.

NO IN AMERICA

Mark Chester

★

Text
GEORGE TOOMER

Foreword
EDWIN NEWMAN

Design
PAUL HOBSON

★

Taylor
Publishing Company

Dallas

Library of Congress
Cataloging in Publication Data

Chester, Mark S.
No in America

1. Photography, Artistic.
2. Signs and signboards—
United States—Pictorial works.
I. Toomer, George. II. Title.

TR654.C483 1986   779′.092′4   86-5956
ISBN 0-87833-539-0

Conceived and produced by Mark Chester
Photographs by Mark Chester
Design by Paul Hobson

photograph of Mark Chester by Lola Troy Fiur
© 1986
Editor: Robert Frese

Printed in the United States of America

0 9 8 7 6 5 4 3 2 1
First Edition

To my loving and generous parents
who never said no.
And to Pamela who said maybe.

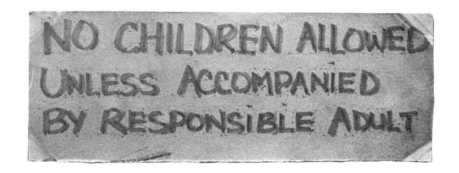

It can be argued that the most important word in the English language is *no*. *Yes* would have its adherents, of course, and *yes* and *no* might be said to be really the same word, since we could not have one without the other. Perhaps they could be called variations on a theme. In any case, trying as life may sometimes be with them, it would be impossible without them.

I cannot prove this, but it seems to me that *no* plays a larger and larger part in our lives. As our numbers increase, as we live closer together and our existence becomes more technological and complicated, the number of things that we must not do inexorably rises. The number of places where we must not do them increases, as well.

The United States will never have more *"No"* signs than people; the country will not become a forest of semiotic prohibitions. There is nonetheless a remarkable profusion of signs warning us that we must not do this or that, and although many of them are routine — *No Parking, No Radio Playing in the Park* (a blessed sign, that) — a good many are not. In some way, those that are not routine reveal something about our country, for they are often expressions of independence, of individuality, sometimes deadly serious, sometimes whimsical, now and then crotchety, occasionally the result of someone's desire to make himself known and to have something to say about what goes on.

There are signs that are really a form of law-making. They did not go through the legislative process, and their constitutionality has never been tested. Still, they exist, and they help to define the limits of what may and may not be. I remember going to California for the first time, in the summer of 1960, and coming upon a sign in the Los Angeles Airport that said, *"No Bare Feet On Escalators."* I had seen a fair part of the United States at the time, and a good part of the rest of the world, but never before had I seen such a ban. Nowhere else, apparently, was it needed. In a sense, that sign said "California" as surely and as plainly as the freeways did, or Hollywood did.

I have a particular fondness for the word *no,* although not, as I try to make clear above, because I prefer it to *yes*. I don't. They are both marvelous words, short, clear, unequivocal models of their kind. Perhaps *no* has a slight edge over *yes*. It does have one fewer letter. It can be put to splendid use:

"Would you agree, sir, that given the circumstances prevailing at this time, and the clear need for this approach, and the number of distinguished citizens who have declared themselves in favor of it, as well as the unmistakeable public demand, now reaching its peak and amounting to a veritable groundswell, and bearing in mind the great benefits that would inure to the nation if we go ahead along the lines indicated, that the recommended swift and determined action, without temporizing or delay, is imperatively called for?"

"No."

Not a bad reply. Not that *no* is always pleasant to hear. It isn't. Still, even in the worst case, with *no* you know where you are, or aren't. You may not like it there, but the position is unambiguous, as it is, for example, in the spiritual *"No Hidin' Place 'round Here."* Another example: the sign *No Exit* is informative and helpful. As the title of a play, indeed as a comment on life, it is powerful and ominous. Or there is that brisk Britishism, *"No, thank you very much."* And its slightly taunting American equivalent: *"Thanks a lot, but no thanks."*

There are many *no's,* the thundering, the defiant, the fearful, the matter-of-fact, the flat, the plaintive, the insinuating, the inquiring, the tearful and pleading, the dismissive, the absent-minded, the futile, the gallant, and who can say how many more. What Mark Chester has done is let his photographer's eye, his mind's eye, wander over the country, to remind us of the part that *no* plays in our lives. It would be possible to impose a pattern on these *no's* and, recalling a best seller of days gone by, label it the power of negative thinking. I'm not sure that would be worth doing. It is the miscellaneity of these *no's* that is their most endearing and revealing quality.

No can be marvelously eloquent. *"No kidding"* says a great deal in two words. *"No strings"* needs no elaboration, though Richard Rodgers did once provide it in a song: "No strings, and no connections, My decks are cleared for action." The rhyme left something to be desired.

Look at the pronouncement, familiar from melodrama, "No, no, a thousand times no!" it is six words long, and three of them are *no.* With how many other words could that be done? With *yes,* of course. Maybe with *perhaps.* Perhaps with *maybe.* That's the list.

"No way" recently has come into popular use: "Will you be taking your sister to the game this afternoon?" "No way." The use is sometimes not grammatical—"No way I'll be there"—but this is another of those terms that catch on because they are terse and definitive: *No show. No fault. No free lunch.* And could there be a more economical description of a baseball player than "Good field, no hit?" Or of a place it would be unwise to go than "No man's land"? *No way* could we get on without them.

I've mentioned "No Strings." The fact is that *no* does not do much for songwriters. There is a resounding *"No, no"* that comes midway through the Prologue to "I Pagliacci," just after the lines in which Leoncavallo, who was his own librettist, suggests (he is setting up a straw man, or in Italian, *uomo di paglia*) that actors do not have real life problems of their own. In "Tosca," the villainous Scarpia, Rome's chief of police, arranges to have Tosca listen as her lover, a painter but more important a tenor, is tortured in the next room. Will he yield the information? It is a groan as much as it is a sung note, but it is also a *no.* Then there is "Rigoletto," in which Rigoletto, preparing to exult over the body of the Duke of Mantua, who has dishonored Rigoletto's daughter, finds that the hired killer has murdered the daughter instead. *"No!"* cries Rigoletto. *"No!"* To, it need hardly be said, *no avail.*

Among writers of popular songs, however, *no* has yielded almost nothing, once you get past Vincent Youmans' "No, No, Nanette"—which has come down to us as the name of a show, not of a song—the Rodgers-Hammerstein "No Other Love," and the Harry Warren-Leo Robin "No Love, No Nothin'," which was what the girls left behind in World War II were to have until their babies came home. Can anyone whistle a bar or remember a line from "No, No, Nora," "No, Not Much," "No One But Me," "No One Ever Loved You More Than I," "No Other Arms, No Other Lips," "No Two People," or "No Wedding Bells For Me"?

There was, it is true, "I'm Just a Girl Who Cain't Say No," Ado Annie's somewhat equivocal lament in Rodgers and Hammerstein's "Oklahoma." Ado Annie was not given to second thoughts, unlike The Lady in "The Lady's 'Yes'," by Elizabeth Barrett Browning:

"Yes," I answered you last night;
"No," this morning, sir I say;
Colors seen by candlelight
Will not look the same by day.

Unlike Mrs. Browning, some writers of other days made great play with the idea that girls would not say *no,* because they wanted to continue leading men on. This was Martial's view almost two millenia ago:

You ask what a nice girl will do? She won't give an inch, but she won't say no.

There was also the belief that if they did say *no,* they didn't really mean it, but said it out of a sense of propriety, or out of coyness. Thus Shakespeare in "Two Gentlemen of Verona":

Since maids, in modesty, say "No" to that
Which they would have the proferrer construe "Yes."

That the girls might have said *no* because they found the men in the case entirely resistible seems not to have been considered. Still, nobody would deny that *no,* spoken with a certain inflection, can mean *yes.* Nor would anyone deny that *no* is remarkably versatile. It can be inspiring. Think of *"No retreat"* as a battlecry. Or *"No surrender."* It can be reassuring: *No problem. No purchase necessary. No sweat.* In food: *No sugar added. No salt. No preservatives. No artificial anything.*

It has its political uses. *"No nukes"* was a catchy slogan, even if its adherents did not prevail. *"No taxation without representation"* was more effective. For that matter, leaving politics behind, the Ten Commandments may be thought of as a collection of *no's.*

One *no* I miss is the *no* in *"No comment."* That was in common use in Washington, and elsewhere, in the 1930's, 40's, and 50's, and a useful phrase it was. Winston Churchill, in Washington for a meeting with President Truman in February 1946, said, "I think, 'No comment' is a splendid expression. I am using it again and again. I got it from Sumner Welles." (Welles was Undersecretary of State at the time.)

Granted that "No comment" was not much help to reporters; you can't write many stories beginning "President So-and-so today declined comment on published reports that..." and those you do write are not likely to be prominently played. All the same, politicians in those days often said "No comment," and nobody thought ill of them for it. It was, I believe, President Kennedy who changed that. He regarded news conferences as contests, and also as opportunities to demonstrate his grasp of affairs. It was almost as though he though it shameful to say "No comment."

Since then, the phrase has largely disappeared from use, with the rambling, unresponsive reply often put in its place. A "No comment" now would be exhaustively analyzed, he who gave it would be subjected to amateur psychiatric examination by columnists, and the pollsters would rush about trying to determine whether the "No comment" had adversely affected his "image" and "performance rating."

I'm sorry to see "No comment" go. Evidently the public relations experts who run today's political campaigns believe that it reflects haughtiness and a lack of the magic ingredients, compassion and concern.

Other *no's* have also taken their departure. *No soap,* meaning "It can't be done," is one. *No organ grinders* is another. There are no organ grinders. *No hawkers* is a third. We now say *No soliciting,* or more bluntly, *No salesmen.* Also *No tickee, no washee,* a not altogether unaffectionate portrayal, in four words, of the immigrant Chinese laundryman telling you that you won't get your laundry back unless you present your ticket.

No can be used sententiously. William James said, "Tell him to live by yes and no — yes to everything good, no to everything bad." As advice, this is too pat to be useful. Ignazio Silone was more helpful when he defined liberty as including "the possibility of saying 'No' to any authority."

More broadly, Nietzsche said, "One must separate from anything that forces one to repeat No again and again." The French writer, Antoine St. Exupery, said, "He who never says 'No' is no true man." Another Frenchman, Alain Chartier, said, "To think is to say no." The people this book examines lean to the St. Exupery and Chartier side.

Edwin Newman, New York, 1986

no (no) *adv.* **1.** Not so. Used to express
refusal, denial, or disagreement.
—*n., pl.* **noes.** **1.** A negative response.
2. A negative vote or votes.
—*adj.* **1.** Not any, not one, not at all.

American
Indian: NEETHAGA

German: NEIN

Old German: NIX

French: NON

Russian: NYET

Spanish: NO

Italian: NO

Hebrew: LO

Gypsy: NU

Chinese: BOO

While the word YES seems to change with every language, our old friend NO seems to be about the same the world over; unfortunately, it generally indicates a lack of fun to most people. In our own language it occupies one of those wonderful positions that allows it to be a noun, an adverb, or an adjective... just to be sure it gets the message across. NO is a very old word that probably originates in the ancient Hindu-Sanskrit... at any rate, it can be communicated with a side-to-side head shake just about everywhere.

The power of the no word has varied through the centuries. No understatement. No doubt a NO from a bigwig in the Spanish Inquisition carried more weight than a NO from our present day evangelists. For my part, I can only establish the power of that famous negative word in today's time in relation to my sphere of influence. Being a WWII baby of 1942, I do have a five year edge on the much acclaimed "Baby Boomers" (1947-53). For this reason I address most of my words towards these people from the position of social critic, not to mention the fact that I enjoy saying NO to those who are younger than I. Inasmuch as this group constitutes the greatest single number of people who have ever lived, and since older is justifiably considered wiser, I become an authority by default... NO EXPERIENCE REQUIRED. ★

An art student goes to school for years. He studies in Italy, France, and Spain. He paints 12 hours a day, seven days a week to perfect his art and understanding of the delicate balance of color, yet his best piece of work, painted with the hand-picked hairs of the rare shrew, dipped in handmade pigment derived from a clay found only in the mountains of Tibet and applied to pure linen canvas woven by virgin novice nuns in a 600 year old convent, won't be as valuable as a cocktail napkin with a doodle by Elvis Presley. Why is that? What makes us have such low standards when it comes to that which enriches our culture?

It's been said that Americans rarely produce culture but they have fine-tuned the selling of culture. My guess is that the literature, art, and music mavens only rise to the level that's demanded by an undemanding public, which thrives on naively optimistic or morbidly fascinating material. A "Jack the Ripper" book outsells books on acid rain or fluorocarbons' effect on the atmosphere and a "Winning Through Intimidation" will outsell books on reforming

workaholics or stamping out the stressful "Type A Behavior."

The packaging and selling of non-stuff is destroying this country. Cheap posters have replaced original art... and even worse, these posters are usually advertising for tourists, clothes, or street art shows for starving artists! You won't see "Starving Writers Shows," which would have stalls full of non-published manuscripts or short stories, because nobody reads anymore. You can buy photographs, you can cherish calligraphy, or collect antique metal type fonts as paperweights... you can even see those damned type trays, where they used to store type for BOOKS,

which are now full of important knick-knacks. Yet, if there is a book sale you can bet it will feature the dreaded non-books. "The Fashions of Lady Di," "Jane Fonda Workouts," "The Art of Verbal Defense," or how some flat-headed Yuppoid dumped his family, friends, and ethics to make a million dollars buying up poor people's houses and selling them back for half the write-off. "NO BOOKS!"

If crummy books didn't sell they wouldn't be printed. The "Readersheep" call the shots. It's they who care about "Private Lives of the Stars" or biographies of famous killers or suicides. There is no mystery about becoming an author these days. It's simply marketing non-books to non-readers, the 70/30 publishing formula. Seventy percent pictures and thirty percent text (large type or huge quotes) in coffee-table size (bigger is better), a slick print book that will reflect the owner's taste in subjects, such as "French Country Cottages," to those who are sitting in the living room, bored stiff, while waiting for the host or hostess to get dressed.

You want to be an author? You want to get in the great stream of the published word? Hell, I'll give these to you free: "Shopping with Adolf & Eva: The WWII Closet of Infamy," "Bastard Blues: The Lives of Illegitimate Children of the Stars," "Trash for Cash: Selling the Garbage of Notables." Since the Baby Boomers call the shots, you should start right now with books such as "Sexy Sixties," "First Signs: The Book for Self-Diagnosis," "Outjogging the Grim Reaper," "Grand Scam...Living off Your Grandparents' Money."

The only good thing about today's literary offerings is the fact that there are so many to pick from. Readersheep are easily bored and will stop buying as soon as the next trend comes along...like taped books, so we don't even need to turn the pages or figure out punctuation. Instead of books we'll have a whole new industry called "Hears." Frankly, I'm glad. I want Readersheep to stay home so they won't be filling up the book store aisles looking at pictures from "The Bermuda Triangle." NO BROWSING!

In fact, I think all books should be sealed (like porno) with an outline on the front. This would wipe out picture books and the coffee table industry. The effect would be startling: apartment living would change as the whole concept of modular bookshelves and magazine racks would be altered. Wall space would return, possibly requiring art as a replacement. Or contemporary novels. Or history. The need for a stereo as background for picture-book flipping would diminish, leaving space for items such as musical instruments. Imagine that, people would actually return to playing music.

Even more important, people might even return to talking about what they have read, if they were bold enough to buy a real book (one rarely hears people discussing picture books as ideas). If you want to know about America as it now stands, there is NO time to waste: READ. As a suggestion only, read "Galapagos," read "Forrest Gump," read "The Underground Empire," read the countless great contemporary writers who should and must be heard: Raymond Carver,

PLEASE NO COMIC BOOK READING

Bobbie Anne Mason, Tom McGuane, William Kennedy, Saul Bellow, and all their many friends and enemies. Just, please, read.

Okay! The switchboard is lit up with people who want to tell me I'm a literary snob. You're right. I feel there are important ideas to be learned from books. Throughout recorded time, there have been those who suggest answers to most of life's problems such as: How to live with your fellow man, How to find happiness when it comes along (or at least how to recognize it), How to produce something good for the world rather than how to take from the world. So I'm an idealistic fool, I live in a dream world.

You bet! I'm tired of a bunch of people saying, "No dreams." People say I'm cynical and negative because I focus on the cynical and nega-

tive. If I wasn't optimistic this would be a book about saving your ass in the inflationary '80s or how to get to Heaven when The Rapture comes after the total destruction of the world by fiery atomic bombs and the forces of evil. Talk about negative, NO DOOM SPEAKERS!

Frankly, I'm getting tired of the current book craze of biographies no one cares about, physical fear books, money management books for the greedies, soul-searching books by those who think they've found the soul, brookeshieldsy books on reality, and anything remotely akin to Hitler, World War II, Rommel, arms, planes, or victory at sea. Did you ever notice there are few books in "People Magazine" on great peace movements or days that nobody fought? Just because the public wants it doesn't mean someone has to publish it!

If the popular trend turns, at it has, toward shooting off our toes, will we be seeing how-to books on mutilation? I think the publishing business is being run by a bunch of ex-photographers and retired fashion models… people living vicariously off the deeds of others.

I'm glad booksellers stack the latest Best Sellers in big stacks so I'll know where they are and be able to find the better stuff in the other end of the store. In fact, that's why I like used book stores, where there are shelves full of books most people don't want. They're usually the best kind. NO NO BOOKS! ★

Books told "NO" by American censors:

CATCH 22
FOREVER AMBER
SLAUGHTERHOUSE FIVE
DELIVERANCE
SHORT STORIES BY NEGRO WRITERS
AMERICAN HERITAGE DICTIONARY
AMERICA IN LEGEND
THE BELL JAR
DADDY WAS A NUMBERS RUNNER
IN THE NIGHT KITCHEN
OF MICE AND MEN
CATCHER IN THE RYE
OUR BODIES OUR SELVES
THE LIVING BIBLE
THE ADVENTURES OF HUCKLEBERRY FINN
TO KILL A MOCKINGBIRD
THE GRAPES OF WRATH
DEATH OF A SALESMAN

THE BOOK OF LISTS
FANNY HILL
WALT WHITMAN's LEAVES OF GRASS
JOYCE's ULYSSES
TROPIC OF CANCER
THE AFRICAN QUEEN
A FAREWELL TO ARMS
TALES OF THE SOUTH PACIFIC
PETER PAN
THE PEOPLE'S ALMANAC

NO
PRE
PACKAGED
PHILOSPHY
ALLOWED

THINK

Most of us learned at a very early age that the impassioned intensity of denial in the word NO, on the lips of parents, teachers, or other adult figures, was in exact proportion to the amount of fun being denied. Therefore, the best swimming holes had the biggest NO SWIMMING signs. If the magic word was screamed by an adult as his face turned red and veins stuck out, you could be assured that you were being kept from childhood Nirvana. We all knew that school halls were, by far, the best places to run and the boy's restroom was the best place to smoke. Certainly, my best place to "park" was that small point of land at the lake from which one could see the Park Patrol a full minute before they could reach your car. I might also add, as an indication of personal revelations to come, that I needed the full minute, because that was the exact time it took to button Alice Fletcher's blouse and get the fuzzy rabbit-collar back in place.

As a mental exercise, one might wonder why there isn't a big push for a resounding NO concerning things the majority of us find offensive like, NO BROCCOLI or NO AUNTS WITH STICKY LIPSTICK or a Saturday with NO JEHOVAH'S WITNESSES. It constantly amazes me that we rarely find people who practice the same vehemence in the denial of hardcore transgressions like toxic waste while spending a lifetime defending a patch of ground with a NO FILL DIRT sign.

My guess is that the word NO gained its power from the fact that it carries so much social clout yet can be transmitted with a simple grunt that requires absolutely no literacy. This gives a cretin the same momentary power as a college professor. In fact, I'm sure I've heard my faithful friend at the zoo, Koto the Gorilla, articulate more in a NO grunt than the woman at the auto title desk.

I learned at a very early age that the failure to recognize the "magic word" could quickly lead to extreme pain in my gluteus maximus or a small lump on my temporalis caused by a dreaded finger thump, or worse, a tablespoon. Even words in the same sound range, such as GO, SO, and OH would stop me in my tracks long enough to take stock of the situation. The brain's capacity to compute the consequences of an action in a split second is fascinating: pleasure is the absence of pain.

Only after years of conditioning did I reach the shaky point at which I would question the authority of the signal. A NO from my friend's mother wouldn't start the adrenaline flowing, while a hint of the word on my grandfather's tobacco-stained lips would immediately cause my foot to draw up. From kindergarten until about the fourth grade I could be numbed with a NO. After that it would only bring a grin to my face, a facial expression that, incidentally, would cost me eleven jobs in the years to come. Oddly enough, I also learned that as a kid NO was a word I couldn't use. It was a word one didn't read coming from Dick or Jane…it simply wasn't in the child's accepted vocab-

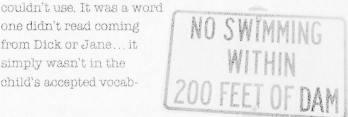

NO FILL MATERIAL ALLOWED
BY ORDER OF PARK CITY MUNICIPAL CORP.

ulary. The constant denial of that delicious word made it all the sweeter on my tongue.

Of course, I was told NO 36 times a day for 19 years by parents, teachers and religiously afflicted authorities, with a continuation of the practice by bankers, government officials, girl friends, and people at the gas company for the 24 years that followed, and I certainly haven't proven YES to be of any cosmic value. I have, however, developed and refined the proverbial "duck's back" method of survival. ★

Could the power of the NO word in one's childhood affect one's direction and determination in saying YES as proof of adulthood and superiority over one's parents? Could the concept of NO actually be one of the driving forces that causes success? Could it be that the greater the awareness of NO as a child, the more you'll try to prove YES when you grow up? There are no answers. ★

When it comes to many NO signs, we may see the apparent need to state a message, but could a giant underlying anger be present? Coming totally out of left field, I offer the premise that the foundation of world terrorism is an exaggerated inability for a person or small group with a real or imagined gripe to be heard against the roar of a crowd with community interest on their minds. There surely exists that type of person, such as a mad-dog Libyan, who feels ineffectual in the face of actions, standards, or movements that flaunt obvious disregard for his position, changes that would jeopardize his authority, moral codes, or pride of ownership. The need to produce a sensational event — or a simple NO sign — might offer a vent for one's trapped hostility, much the same effect as graffiti. For the price of a Magic Marker, a can of spray paint, or fingernail polish on the cardboard from a laundered shirt, a person can impose his momentary will on all who would take the time to read the often misspelled, scribbled message attesting to the power of "The Little Man." These scrawls offer a warning that the scribe has been pushed to the point of no return.

My guess is that the message sender hopes that offenders will breach the stated contract so that some act of retribution will be justified, an act that will force the world to recognize his plight. This is Lilliputian terrorism, firing tiny darts at the world giant called Indifference. There is no understanding these people.

NO SLEEPING IN VEHICLES OR ON BEACH 6.00 PM TO 6.00 AM
CITY CODE SEC. 639.5 & 639.6

Needless to say, all NO signs aren't the work of crazed personalities. I recognize the need for a certain number of do and don't directionals: NO SWIMMING near a whirlpool, NO DIVING in a rock quarry, and NO SMOKING in a fireworks factory. But my brain goes into Mach 2 when I see NO TANK TOPS, or NO FACIAL HAIR.

One of my personal puzzlements is nightclubs and spiffy eateries with those little brass signs on the door stating NO JEANS or, in the affirmative, PROPER ATTIRE REQUIRED. This means a person wearing a $150 pair of custom jeans (made by Italian Virgins), a $200 pure silk shirt, and those $300 Italian designer shoes that last about two weeks will be turned away, while a guy in a $69 Sear's suit, $16 Penney's shirt, and a Disneyland tie will be admitted. I actually don't give a flip about either one of these people, nor would I go to a place that didn't feature "take-out," but the issue remains. A salute to pettiness: Little minds make big signs. ★

In a country jam-packed with terminal "Candoism," celestial Dale Carnegie courses, and daily messages from God, it seems incongruent that the word NO would even exist much less control so many of our actions. After all, YES is what this country is all about. YES, you can be rich. YES, everyone can grow up to be president. Hell, ask any high school coach to entertain the possibility of NO when it comes to winning. "This is America, boy! Home of the fighting Wildcats. We got God

and tradition on our side!" To say NO in the face of our prized "Rugged Individualism" is to flirt with danger. We'll defend our right to say YES to the death, if that's what it takes... even if we're wrong.

An interesting rub occurs when a person on a full-tilt course towards fulfilling the need to impose his will on others meets up with an equally righteous person, usually of left brain attitude, who states, "Ain't no son-of-a-bitch gonna tell me what to do!" This is an important thread in the fabric of a society which creates these mutually dependent extremes. Like a sadist and a masochist wedding, it becomes a dovetailing of neuroses. Would the night club with a fashion code be disappointed if they didn't get to turn anybody away? Their self-image depends on poor dressers.

In most countries we find there is a select group who toy with the meaning of the NO commandments in a pick and choose fashion, much like a moral cafeteria. They place themselves above many of those restrictions most of us are required to live with. Michael Jackson or Prince could easily go into a posh restaurant wearing some dumb glitter coat and no shirt while we must have coat and tie. NO COVER CHARGE! ★

Personally, I fail to see why anyone would shop in a store with a NO sign in the window. To me it's a kiss of death, like when the suffix "-fest" is added to anything (artfest, cityfest, craftfest); it's a guarantee that the event or promotion is put together by keychain and ballpoint pen salesmen or, at least, a soft drink or hotdog company.

When any sign has more than one NO on it, you can bet you're about to visit a store full of macramé, plastic ferns, or a giant Unicorn collection. I feel a NO sign is a little bit like a trick question. If I don't go inside the shop, I'm obviously admitting that I have a tank top on under my shirt, or that I had rather be barefooted, or that my pockets are secretly bulging with loose food. If I do go in, I automatically submit: "You're the boss O' Exalted Potentate and Keeper of all that is Good…and I swear to the Great Fire God of Shopping that I will not cash a personal check or have any bill larger than a dollar after 10:00 P.M." Those signs make me feel like an idiot who doesn't know the rules. "Wait a minute! I don't even smoke. Why do I feel guilty?" ★

I understand terrorism. I don't like it, but I understand it. I hate it and I hate what causes it... self-righteousness, greed, and stupid male-ness. I don't like terrorism on any level, whether it be a bunch of ragheads holding hostages or a pack of religious zealots holding politicians to the fire with threats of marches. I don't like killing innocent people. Why can't terrorists just blow up their equals on the other side? Let soldiers and politicians do each other in and keep civilians out of it. The guy on the street doesn't make bombs. He pays air-conditioning bills, water bills, and gives money to the government so they can make bombs and support a bunch of Yahoos around the world that still like playing "army." NO FIRE-ARMS ON PREMISES!

Did you ever pay close attention to the terrorists that show up on the news? Kids! Teen-agers or people in their early twenties walking around with machine guns. A machine gun in the Middle East is like a BMW or a Polo shirt here... it's the means and end thing, so you can get the chicks. "Well, Abdul, it's time you got a job and did something with your life. Why don't you talk to Abbal the sheep guy and maybe he'll put you on for the summer?" The kid finishes cutting up a sock or ski mask and says, "That's a nerd job, Pop. I want to work with the guys in the Jihad... get my own machine gun, learn explosives, get to travel, meet girls who are willing to die with me." Sotto voce, "Which means that sex is okay because I might not be around next Tuesday."

If you want to put a stop to terrorism in the Middle East I suggest you fly over and drop pamphlets that say: "Young men. Earn big money as manager of a 7-11. Get a free TransAm and your choice of two-tone patent leather shoes or leather jacket for renouncing your organization." The back would feature a picture of a semi-clad American blonde.

We know how dumb American kids are at eighteen when they have a march of protest to change the school mascot. One can just imagine the fervor of Irish or Eastern youth when they see all the hoopla and glory surrounding some buddy who blew himself up while mishandling a bomb. Rarely do we hear of a guy in his fifties get-ting blasted. Kids love glory and romanticism... let 'em do the work. In fact, romance might be the actual fuel of the revolution. Romantics and mystics are known for all those mushy poems and crybaby stories where the hero always ends up with a broken heart or all blown up... remem-ber Gunga Din? (India guy. Same basic area.) NO BLEEDING HEARTS!

I don't like the Middle East either. They do bad things to women and they're always out in the road shaking their fists... they remind me of Fire Ants. Don't these people have jobs? But, of course, what kind of job could you have if you had to bow to Mecca five times a day? I'd hate to be in surgery over there at sundown. ★

While following a woman who had obviously turned over her driving fate to God, I noticed her bumper sticker which read, "Honk if you love Jesus!" Boy, I bet that sits well in Heaven, knowing the supposedly most important name in the world is just above the exhaust pipe of a '68 Chevy Belair, stacked full of used Early American furniture and brass pole lamps. NO BUMPER STICKERS!

I get tired of people who allow some stranger to write their personal creeds for them. SAVE THE WHALES, U.S. OUT OF U.N., I SAW WONDER CAVE. Who cares? If you have something you think is important, why not write it yourself? Get a crayon or Magic Marker and some sticky paper and be original, at least.

The real problem with bumper stickers is you are limited to the number of things you can be concerned about. Since most stickers are 3½" x 12" and most car bumpers are approximately 4½ feet wide, you can only be passionate about four issues... or three if your license plate is in the middle of your bumper. What about couples who don't agree? Would she have NO NUKES on her side of the bumper while he has KILL A COMMIE FOR CHRIST on his? If he's a right-winger must he have his sticker on the right side of the car? What if one has a change of heart on an issue? Do you cover up the old sticker with a new statement? If one is wishy-washy then we might find a multi-layer stack of bumper stickers.

Red is the worst color for use in the sun... it fades. Since lowbrow people produce most of the bumper stickers, they tend to use a lot of red ink. We often see bumper stickers reading, "Don't blame Jesus if you go to _____" (the last word has faded). If these same people are travelers they might have another sticker next to it for an amusement park, so we see a complete message: "Don't blame Jesus if you go to Sea World." NO SHTICK! ★

The other day I was reminded about why I love my particular lifestyle. In an elevator I was accosted by a young guy in corporate attire. "It must be nice to run around in Hawaiian shirts, blue jeans, and to have a beard." I assured him that it was a very natural, live-for-the-moment sort of thing. We discussed my full beard, which I told him required nothing to produce. The usual question that I ask myself: Why would a person spend the majority of his or her life dressed uncomfortably or in clothes that one hates? To make money is the usual answer.

I think the only people who actually enjoy wearing a barrister's suit or a necktie are the people who get to inflict such a uniform on others by establishing a dress code that requires such conformity, like at IBM. Bosses, supervisors, and people with sour dispositions, I'll bet. Anal retentives who fear chaos caused by anything different. People who hang their clothes exactly three inches apart and roll their underwear in six inch lengths... people who complain about eggs not being over-easy enough or Martinis that aren't dry enough. Wimps! Sticks in the mud!

I've noticed a new trend among the "Biz-guys and Gals": Mercantile Macho. A style that has one being proud of suffering for the cause. Not only do we see buttoned-down shirts, buckled-down shoes, snap-down collars, lock-down watches, and Velcro'd billfolds, but now there's a movement towards suspenders (called "braces" by Biz-zealots). Like a "Sam Brown" belt, suspenders do nothing but keep your pants crotch tight... they must like that. Another trend has people going back to white shirts as proof they are "More biz minded than thou" and willing to suffer any discomfort in the name of success. NO ALL WHITES!

I think this swing back in time is designed to make people recognizable to each other. God help you if you're a closet print-pattern shirter!

Maybe the plan is to be damned sure you're "white collar" and not blue collar. Could we be seeing a national movement towards "collarization?" Bankers, insurance agents, investors, software people, and heavy corporate types will wear only white collars. Architects, planners, engineers, and designer types will wear plaid or print collars. Anybody that works with their hands, backs, or feet will be blue collar, while liberals, eggheads, teachers, writers, artists, musicians, shrinks, or anybody that comes close to intellectual status must wear a Day-glo red collar for easy identification. Minorities, longhairs, or guys with beards will be excluded because they are easily recognized as troubled people.

What gets me is the smugness of white-shirters. They love to pull off their blazers or solid-color suit coats and "get down" at lunch or any other public place. I noticed it first in political advertising. The media consultants tell the future presidents, "Pull off your coat and throw it over your shoulder. Be one of the guys. Look casual but professional." I think they do it to impose their will on a crowd like a priest with a collar. When one's in the area, we can't swear, spit, or break wind, and no talking about sex or being silly. One must pay proper respect to higher things like God... or money, in the case of the white-shirters. NO FUN! ★

REX STAINED GLASS STUDIOS
MAIN STREET
WEST STOCKBRIDGE, MA. 01266

NO BARE FEET
NO BEAR FEET
NO "MY GRANDMOTHER HAD ONE OF THESE."
NO WHITE BELTS

* RESTRICTIONS SUBJECT TO CHANGE WITHOUT NOTICE

Should you be required to obey a NO sign that is incorrect or misspelled? When a sign reads NO DANCEING or VIOLETERS WILL BE PROZIQUTED what are we to do? To honor such a statement would be to laugh in the face of concise law and order. We will not be controlled by misinformation!

What about signs that instruct me to avoid actions I don't even understand, such as, NO WHEELIES or NO CHIPPING or NO FEET for God's sake. I'm in double jeopardy right off with my 10½ D's. Could you possibly carry your own sign? For instance, could I walk into a store that had a sign in the window stating NO MUSLE SHIRTS while carrying my sign that reads NO MISSPELLING and force the owner to remove his sign?

Since the world seems to recognize the enforceability of NO signs, I wonder how far we could push the point? For

example, could we have a set of signs that we carry in our cars? NO TAILGATING, NO LANE SWITCHING WITHOUT A SIGNAL, or NO GRAVEL TRUCKS WITHIN 1000 FEET. We might come close to the outer limits with NO POLICE UNIFORMS. ★

There are a few NO signs that I would like to see:

NO LIME GREEN GOLF PANTS
NO POODLES
NO UGLY BUILDINGS
NO WAR
NO RATE HIKES
NO UNICORNS
NO LONG SPEECHES
NO SPORTS TALK
NO LIVER
NO GUILT TRIPS
NO HEALTH FREAKS
NO DEVELOPERS
NO EXTREME MAKEUP JOBS
NO TURNIP GREENS
NO CHEAP CIGARS
NO SALES MOTIVATION SEMINARS
NO PREACHERS WITH WIGS
NO PERFECTIONISTS
NO TOFU
NO PEOPLE WHO LOOK BETTER THAN ME
NO PINK HAIR
NO RICH TEENAGERS
NO UGLY SPICE RACKS
NO REAL ESTATE PITCHES
NO CAR PHONING IN TRAFFIC
NO PHONE SOLICITORS

Have you noticed that the need for heavy-handed information signs has increased as humans, supposedly, are getting smarter? Very few NO signs have been found in cave dwellings of primitive man, while our current condo clusters have dozens of signs concerning parking, swimming, and laundry room rules. Social evolution.

What will the situation be in another 500 years? My guess is that we'll have to learn codes. NO PARKING might be 12, while NO FEET might be 99. NO PETS could be 62, and maybe NO FISHING would be a 25. Therefore, one sign reading 12-99-62-25 would either cover a bilateral

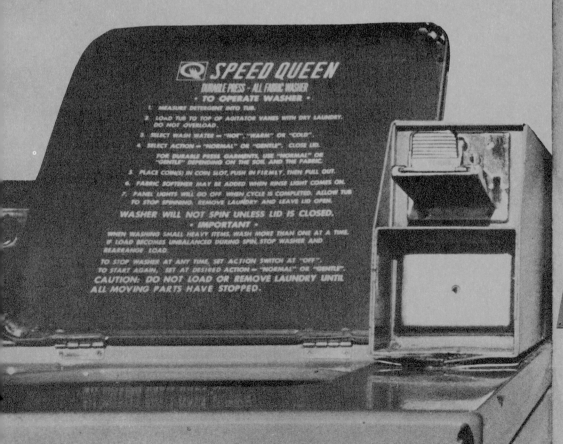

amputee making out with his girl while his cat is
slashing at goldfish or it might mean NO STOP-
PING YOUR CAR AND STANDING ON THE RAIL
WHILE USING A POODLE FOR SHARK BAIT. ★

It doesn't take a steel-trap mind to see that certain situations and social conditions seem to call for NO signs more than others. For instance, businesses near tourist attractions, high schools, and major freeway exits seem to be the target of groups with the mentality that requires constant direction and attention. The owners of these shops and stores, under siege, often become an extremely threatened group. Their cry reflects endless encounters with the mindless masses who feel they have a singular, personal right to extraordinary service, because they have a little extra money and free time. The NO signs are usually directed at the immature, the rude, and the irrational, who lean toward instant gratification with little thought about the wishes of others.

We have an interesting study in social evolution when we look at people on vacation and the people who serve them. Let rain collect in a two-foot puddle and tourists will swim in it. Let a pile of rubble reach hip height and it becomes Mt. Everest to a touring child. When vacationers get on the road, some of them revert to a childlike state of wonderment that has them climbing, crawling, and jumping on things they would never notice in their real lives. An accountant who lives in a white shirt with a tie and only experiences danger in the form of pencil lead poisoning and paper cuts will suddenly jump off a rock cliff or hang upside down on a giant oak limb the minute he puts on a Hawaiian shirt. His need to cram as much excitement as possible into 72 hours overrides his sense of reality, thus the need for that gentle reminder of potential broken bones or, more importantly, a hole in his checkbook. When these people get out of their natural waters, they leave all their cares behind. NO CARE!

For me, economic life is pretty simple. I work, get my money, and pay my bills. I'll refer to my married days to make this work. The order of things seemed to be that I paid out money based on priorities that were good for me and my family. 1. Shelter; 2. Food; 3. Utilities; 4. Telephone; 5. Transportation; 6. Credit cards which cover clothing, some household items, business entertainment, some food, etc.; 7. Insurance; 8. Medical bills; and so on... political contributions are up around 163 and religious contributions are 1,437 (right after handouts to retired circus clowns). If I don't have any money left at the end of payments, I usually go without until I get in better shape. I put all items in priority, i.e., I would never refuse to give my son a hot lunch so that I could spend the money impressing a customer with an extra Scotch on the rocks. I would never loan a friend a buck, if it meant that we would be eating soda crackers. I know, pretty close, the amount I will have next year, so I don't take out a loan I can't pay just so that my financial picture will look good on paper... so I can borrow more money. My lenders won't fall for that.

Now I look at the national debt: Even though I know that America is not a company, I feel it should be run on the same tight schedule as a money maker. I'm sure that there are many who currently agree. The problem is who judges the extras? The country is actually a giant household with a family of two hundred thirty seven million, two hundred thousand (at last count), with a couple of hundred thousand added every hour or so.

To explain a point, I will break it down into a microcosm of the mythical Wally family. A few hundred years ago great, great, great Grandfather Horace Wally made it big and left his descendants all his wealth. His immediate family got more than his distant relations. This wealth has been passed down accordingly. Grandpa Wally is still alive and metes out the real money to his many children. They all think about the day when he will die and they will have control over all the cash. There is Fred Wally, who took his money and invested in real estate so all his family does pretty good. Next we have Vernon Wally, who wanted to farm; Max Wally, who was born with no arms or legs; Wanda Wally, who stays to herself with all her kids who help in the cafe; Bubba Wally, who is retarded and likes to play army at the age of 42; Bubba's favorite Uncle Hank, who has been in the Army for 28 years and was decorated on Iwo Jima; Mindy and Mae Wally, who own a few restaurants and hotels (one on Park Place) and

wish to marry the Dobson twins who own a bunch of land down near the freeway.

The dark sides of the family are Billy, who went crazy in Korea and has lost sixteen jobs; Rocky, the burglar, who's in and out of the slammer; and Freda Wally, who has such low self-esteem that she sleeps with the guys in the fleet who promise to marry her next time they're in town…leaving her with seven kids. The bright side of the family are the young who are not yet as negative as the grownups, but have variations of their hangups. The young are afraid that the elders are wasting the family fortune and making deals that they, the kids, will have to pay for. They haven't had the triumphs or the heartaches of the older generation. The concept of war means nothing and many of the kids feel that the end of the world is near because Uncle Silas, a religious zealot, scared them all at the family picnic. Uncle Silas is in his later years and he's afraid of death.

So how does the Wally family handle the money? Grandpa Wally says they should pool the funds and write checks according to need. Fred suggests they invest more to assure future fortune for the family.

Right up front, Bubba starts ranting about attacks from mysterious forces who want to bring the family to ruin. In fact, he spouts, there are members of the Wally family who want it to fail! "We must have somebody watch them every minute and report back, just in case!" he says. He continues, "If you don't put them under surveillance, I ain't gonna vote for your real estate deals!"

Col. Hank chimes in, "We had a bunch of turncoats back in the big war in '41 and they were bad cookies... even hid secret messages in the movies that were bad for morale." Bubba is happy for the support from Uncle Hank.

"Well, we got a budget here," says Grandpa, "But we'll hire a couple of guys to watch things so you'll feel comfortable in your bed, Bubba."

Col. Hank sees how easy it was so he takes a chance. "If those guys find out there's family enemies, we'll need soldiers to protect the house here... so just in case, we should hire a bunch and train 'em. They'll need a house to stay in as well."

Bubba adds, "We need an alarm system... in fact I know some guys over in Smithville who could tell us if they see any bad guys coming. They'll do it for a small fee!"

As the idea catches on, Col. Hank joins in. "Hell, let's just put some of our guys over in Smithville and we can fight 'em out of town, so the womenfolk will be safe!"

The conversation continues until Vernon says, "Things ain't going well at the farm and if you expect me to keep feeding the family I'm gonna have to get some new equipment and what about Max? He's got no arms or legs and he needs a nurse to feed him. That costs money."

The battle continues until somebody notices that they have gone over the budget by 275% and they don't have enough to make it. Everybody wants a piece of the pie and is unwilling to give up. Some of the members begin to resent those who can't or won't produce more profit for the family. Before it's over, the profiteers, the speculators, and those who are paranoid have promised money to every Joe Bob who can make them money, or protect them from real or imaginary foes. Finally, young Westly Wally says, "You people are spending our money and we'll get the bill for the rest of our lives and that of our children. Let's simplify by keeping that which does the most realistic good for the family: Health, shelter, food, education, and care for the Infirm, feeble, and aged... if any is left we will buy extras."

The conversation raged into the night with the profit-motivated at one point of the triangle and the paranoid and bleeding hearts on the others. While they fought, Grandpa continued to write checks supporting all that they had requested because life goes on. Each knew that the family was going broke as the money bags

drained. Fred's kids got piano lessons while Wanda's kids had to take summer jobs in his construction company which he thought was very fair... and they worked so cheap. Vernon's kids joined the Army with Uncle Hank because Vernon's farm couldn't produce money for them... Hank was very happy because they worked so cheap. Max died one day when he got caught in the bed sheets... it was for the better. Mindy and Mae married the Dobsons and introduced them to Uncle Fred and after the land deal of the century, both couples divorced with the girls getting a tidy settlement, which they had no intention of adding to the Wally family coffers. So they went abroad in search of exotic lovers and foreign land deals, which they knew Uncle Hank would protect with his soldiers if needed. The family debt just kept getting bigger and everyone concerned

hoped nobody would notice. When the little people in the family squawked, the elders and family heads would suggest a "study" that would continue until the problem cured itself or those concerned forgot while they struggled to survive... and on it went.

I'm sick of the national debt. I'm tired of the talk and politics. NO POLLING WITHIN 100 FEET! I'm fed up with buying 3000 shoes for some jerkwater ruler's wife, while complaining about giving shoes to our own poor. I don't understand how we can continue to bribe countries with aid and arms, while we can cut kid's lunch programs. I don't understand funds for bombers that will go to waste or become outdated while we have raffles to see who gets a kidney transplant. How can we pay for a military marching band and cut money for city orchestras? Why do we need military golf courses? For that matter, why do we need flagpoles when everyone knows what country this is? Why do churches get to own tax-free parking garages, book stores, colleges, recording studios, airplanes, bands, and bingo parlors that compete with us? Why does a guy with 10,000 acres, 10 apartment houses, and a $100,000 quarter horse pay less taxes than a college professor? Why does an arms company make more money than a medicine company? Why do we have to pay for the Air Force Blue Angels flying team to go to air shows? Because Fred Wally and the family like it that way. NO ROCKING THE BOAT! ★

It's easy to pass judgment on others since history gives us a clear picture of what went wrong. I have some pretty strong opinions about events and ideas that would have changed history, but in reality, the only real needs for the NO word are concerned with how NO would have changed MY history. Not that my life will get you on the edge of your seat, but I DO recall some examples that may help us both.

The first incident of NO being required would be titled "The Ice Walk in the Winter of 1944." My first walk on slick ice with my dog, "Pudge, the Chow," ended in total disaster as we both slipped and knocked out our front teeth. I have developed a healthy respect for slick surfaces and bad footing these last 40 years. In fact, I rarely let anything get between my feet and the earth but shoe leather. "Do you ski?" they ask. I look down at my 280-pound frame and just say NO.

Eating paste in Sister Calistus' room (1947) was a clear need for NO that I failed to recognize. Caught red-handed (or gooey-lipped, as the case might be), I was forced to stand in the cloak closet for what seemed to be 73 years. Being an innovative kid, I climbed up on a shelf to rest, only to be confronted with certain doom as Sister C. tried to find me. Not realizing that I was just above her head, she raced around the partition (thinking I was on the other side) trying to catch me. Finally, I jumped down in hopes of diminishing the anger and was immediately grabbed in one of those painful holds that only Sisters of Charity are taught. Even today, I am convinced that they have a target chart of a child that shows all the pain points. I was sentenced to cleaning all the erasers on the second floor (about a million), which I decided to do by dropping them out of the window to see them make "bombs" of chalk dust on the blacktop... not realizing that said dust was being sucked into the basement lunchroom by a fan just below my window, where there was a nunnery meeting in progress. The outcome was three knuckle whacks, a cheek tweak, a screaming reference to my lack of confirmation, a reminder of the disappointment of the Saints, Baby Jesus, Mother Mary, the Pope, and Father Cambell (which really hurt), topped off with a mandatory trip to the chapel where I was instructed to refrain from chewing the varnish off the pew, which was my normal habit.

Another? As my secret and total heart-throb, Mary Lou Hay, watched, I placed an old wooden milk crate firmly in the fork of an elm tree that hung over Merrimac Street. I pretended to fall asleep as she watched and hollered some silly, girlish thing (probably with more intelligence than I would know for the next three years). When I awoke, I was in the arms of Mr. Bleekman with blood running down my face and stars dancing before my eyes. It became obvious that I had bounced a couple of times on the pavement. Everyone stared at me in horror as we walked by. Finally an ambulance came and I was wheeled out of my house in my underwear for all the world, including Mary Lou, to see. It was probably that single act of stupidity that ruined the world of marriage that my nine-year-old mind had created. She became a lasting image of NO.

From the summer of 1956 until the fall of 1957, I simply threw the NO word out the window. During the rites of passage for a young male, there comes a need for instant masculine identity. This can be accomplished with a small growth of lip hair, a motorcycle, or a tattoo. Acting mature is never an option.

I'm not sure who actually turned me on to the mystical secret of self-defacing, but I think it was a guy named Howard who shared detention hall with me. Howard had a series of poorly executed marks on his skinny arm. One was a backward, upside-down "R" (for rebel) and a pirate skull. The "R" probably read correctly to him as he did it... not that Howard could read, mind you. Being an artist, it only seemed natural that I, too, should flaunt my ability. The following process, probably never before recorded by literate man, is simple.

The secret of Home Tattoo is a few household items: two wooden matches (kitchen size),

two medium sewing needles, white thread, a small bottle of India ink and a ballpoint pen or Mom's eyebrow pencil. You must totally suspend logic.

STEP 1. Place needles (2) on either side of a single match with the points about ¼" beyond the tip. Wrap white thread around needles and match toward the points, pulling points together as you wrap (white thread gives you a false sense of sterilization). Just before the points actually touch, loop thread in and out to maintain slight separation.

STEP 2. With your pen or eyebrow pencil, draw design on area to be defaced. A scorpion or initial for men shows toughness, while a butterfly for women offers a gentle touch, if you haven't chosen a motif. Be sure your design is where you want it, actual size and very simple.

STEP 3. Dip needle/match assembly into India ink until thread draws up a good amount of pigment. You are now ready to puncture your skin and create pain and blood. Remember: once you start, there is NO going back. Carefully press needle points until you feel the skin give, letting you know it is broken. Continue this process until you have made a complete outline of your design. You won't actually know if it worked until it heals. Wash it with alcohol and hope for the best. ★

A teenage boy can rarely say NO to girls. I couldn't. Girls who are 16 can be very dramatic, compulsive, emotional, neurotic, sociopathic, self-

centered, attention-starved, and they can lie a little bit. Donna was all the above and, in fact, ran the entire course on a daily basis. When I was in military school (another good time to say NO) she would send me an astounding 7-10 page letter daily, all doused with some type of teen perfume that smelled like Southern Comfort, a fragrance that still causes my throat to close up. Her letters would start off with provocative quips like: "You'll be glad to know that I'm carrying your child," or other delightfully puzzling items such as, "I had a long talk with your mother today...and she agrees!" ★

One should always say NO to registering for anything. They say you might win a sewing machine or a "Mystery Second Prize." In my case, it was a ½-acre of "Prime New Mexico land" only a few feet from the great ski resorts where skiers raced down white powder slopes with rosy faces, according to the slides. It was land often trod by Kit Carson and famous Indian chiefs. I should have questioned it when I realized the land

was a second prize to a sewing machine. But NO-O-O...I wanted to be a land owner. The land was free, according to the guy with "Lucky" tattooed on his knuckles and a giant diamond horseshoe ring. We watched more slides and felt the dirt that was contained in a fishbowl. The only problem was the cost of closing the deal, a process that required cash that must be paid before 12:00 midnight of the same day we received the phone call. My mind said NO while my mouth said YES as I peeled off the crisp bills my wife had so carefully saved. She said NO! to my deaf ear. Later we would read "Life" magazine together as we saw our land for the first time: "Great Land Scandal...100's Bilked as State says: NO WAY.

I could speak of dozens of times I should have said NO in recent times, but they're just too painful...going out with a therapist who wanted me to spank her; using the accountant who always said "No sweat on the small stuff"; or letting a guy named "Knubby" show me how to use power equipment. I think I'll mercifully say NO to more trips down Memory Lane. NO WALLOWING IN THE PAST! ★

NEXT 4 MILES
RESTRICTED AREA
No Swimming No Wading
No Shooting No DOGS
NO ACTS OF POLLUTION
Napa City Water Dept.

Generally, the political power of the NO word shows up in the hands of those who stand to lose something in the face of YES, such as money or authority over those who have a little money or the power to make money. The YES group seems to be comprised of those who don't have the power to make big money…but would like to.

The conservative faction is in a state of "being" while the liberal side is in a constant state of "going to be" as they dream of the world to come. This sets up a trend that has the conservative usually saying NO to ideas and policies that might erode his edge. Of course the other side is screaming YES to any attractive method that will allow them to move up to the next level where the money is. The Right idealistically stands firm on the tried and true while the Left, equally idealistic, wants to keep things stirred up in hopes of making a breakthrough. The Far Right often issues its NO based on the tradition that it finds so comfortable, a comfort usually supported by moral teachings, parental tradition, and a type of blind patriotism stemming from romance and easily charged emotionalism. This is one reason for heavy conservative traits in the South where more Bibles are read to them than read. The Far Left, on the other hand, quickly hollers YES to its idealistic Utopian dreams that would have everyone equally sharing the wealth. Unfortunately,

this liberal dream quickly fades when one realizes that, given equal starts, a hard worker, with motivation, will motivate himself and grow strong while a non-motivated soul will hang around the TV all day and ask the money maker to help him out, then hate the money maker because he's got the power to say NO.

The Left and The Right are both on target when it comes to their respective realities. Spoon in a couple of lumps of self-righteousness, a scoop of Horatio Alger, and a dash of Marx and we have that wonderful social stew that makes our world go around. With flame-red faces, bulging neck veins, and furrowed brows, each side dashes to get the power, if for no other reason than to say NO to the other. I often wonder if each side exists mainly to thwart the other rather than work towards a common goal to benefit all. In fact, it could be that each side might only say YES to really stupid policies in hopes that the other side's failure will prove them right. ★

NO LOITERING OR ELECTIONEERING BETWEEN THIS POINT AND THE POLL

What if Ben Franklin had listened to the doom speakers and never tried to let an electrical discharge of a Leyden jar go across a gap to raise the reading on a thermometer to prove that electricity caused heat? We'd be drying our hair with a piece of burning wood. If Ben hadn't written his thesis on the electrical properties of lightning, the Frenchman D'Alibard wouldn't have stolen the idea and proved him right. Franklin is one of my favorite American men in history. The word NO simply didn't fit into his vocabulary when it came to invention, religious intelligence, and certainly the Post Office that allows me to get hate mail. NO CHARGE!

An 1800's dentist named Horace Wells went up against tons of professional NO's to allow himself to be put under nitrous oxide gas during a tooth extraction by another dentist. "It did not hurt more than the prick of a pin! It is the greatest discovery ever made!" he said on recovery. Horace gets my vote and I'm glad he said YES.

We could pick any number of great people who made contributions to our lives. I could turn this into a historical piece by naming one tenth of them. I will refrain and only mention old C. L. Sholes, surely one of your favorites, too. C. L. said YES to a mechanical device that had a carriage of movable type that moved one click to the left when a letter was printed and the keys worked on a pianoforte action to become the first modern typewriter. A contraption that allows wonderfully creative people, well, not unlike myself, to easily put down a string of words that expose their innermost thoughts to the world, for which they get poorly paid. Thanks, Mr. Sholes!

Edward R. Murrow, the journalist who exposed Joe McCarthy; Margaret Sanger, the leader of the birth control movement (We still don't have enough sense to understand); the nameless protestor of the 1960's who said NO to a useless war that only served to enrich special interests in a wartime economy (Where are you now?); Helen Keller, who said NO to the bonds of handicap... all are heroes of the NO word.

I look back on history in this country and I see a few times I wish somebody had enough sense to say NO. People like Dr. Richard Jordan Gatling, who turned his great ability towards a rapid fire gun that would be the grandfather of the modern day machine gun. This weapon, when used against an advancing enemy, would allow wholesale death and destruction. Of course, many would say that it saved lives in the long run, but I feel that the Gatling Gun was a major step toward mechanized warfare that further dehumanized killing. Realizing that wars are generally fought by comparable types of men, I wish they would be forced to use sticks, teeth, and dirt clods.

While I'm on the subject of saying NO to war, I'll add Dr. J. R. Oppenheimer. There were many scientists involved in the Manhattan Project that fathered the atomic bomb. Dr. Oppen-

DEPARTMENT

OF

TRANSIT AND TRAFFIC

NO NUKES!

CITY OF BALTIMORE

heimer is the convenient choice as its parent. He later had a change of heart and wished he and his cohorts would have said NO to developing the bomb. Again, military-minded knotheads would say it saved lives, but its ability to destroy the world simply isn't worth it, in this book. I respect a warring tribe of Pygmies more than I do our modern armies, because they have the sense not to burn their own jungle in order to win.

Whether it was a financial move, a publicity stunt, or a cost-cutting action, the powers-that-be in the Coca Cola boardroom lost the country's respect with the flip-flop on the original Coke formula. Not that such a thing is important in the scale of life, but rather it was a clear indication of the "New Business Posture" of this country, a state that has put consumers in the saddle for a ride down the rugged manipulation trail. I wish consumers would say NO to corporations who cut quality, content, or size for an extra buck. It's like having accountants in the kitchen who have the job of taking out grains of salt or spice so that the profit will reflect the cut in three years. Somewhere along the line I hope people will finally say, "No sale, pal. A 2-ounce bar of candy isn't worth a buck fifty," or "I'm not going to pay $30,000 for a car that stays in the shop all the time…even if it is a status symbol." NO SHOW OFFS!

Certainly one of the most important times somebody should have said NO was to the remake of "Leave It to Beaver." LITB offered some of the

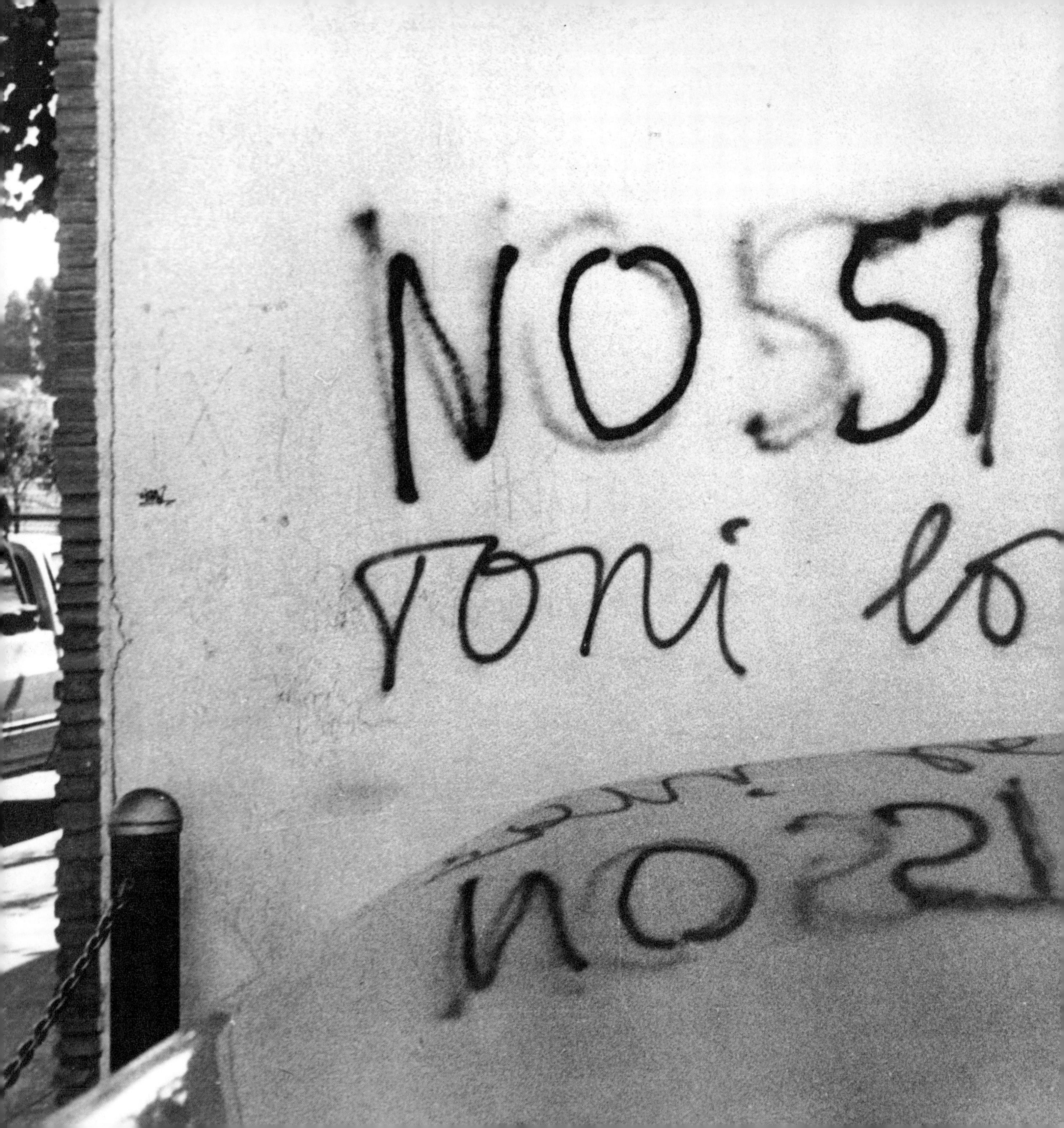
NO ST
Toni lo

finest writing to be found in its original shows. I wish the Beave had said NO and not destroyed the fantasy many of us maintained as we watched reruns. When we see that members of the cast have become policemen, real estate dealers, and such, we will never be able to watch the first shows again without thinking of real life. What if Judy Garland had remade "The Wizard of Oz"... as an adult? What if Laurence Olivier appeared on "Love Boat"? By God, some memories are sacred! NO RETURNS! ★

Rather than the loss of scientific research or the loss of life, I secretly think that the Challenger tragedy upset the powers-that-be because it put a big hickey in the Star Wars program... the so-called defense system in outer space that would have us in "The Empire" position. Of course it would save us money in the long run, because we wouldn't need to have financial clout over Third World countries in order to impose our will on the world. We could simply run a press release about our laser ability in their local newspapers. I am bitter about the money we spend on concepts that hurt rather than help. NO HAZARDOUS MATERIAL!

When I think of "defense," I visualize a paranoid oil man who mentally elevates a poor majority, which must buy chicken necks and pig guts simply to survive, to the point in his imagination of constituting a well-organized army determined ultimately to invade the wealthy side of town to take away his Toro mowers and Rolex watches. He has installed a $300,000 alarm system in a $150,000 house. Rather than go out to the movies, a play, or visit the art galleries, this gentleman chooses to stay home and protect his material items with an arsenal of weapons that could kill every poor person in town. Rather than experience life, he spends his time reading books about how burglars get into houses and all the bad things they can do... a book that is published by the people who manufacture burglar alarms, burglar bars and weapons. On the front

74

of "Survivor Times," "Paranoid Journal," or "Survival Weekly," one can find pictures of the most frightening stereotypes, such as brown guys with rings in their ears, dirty caps and gold teeth, Russian children in military schools, crowds of Iranians shaking their fists, Orthodox Jews with strange hats and ledgers like bullets, black people playing dominoes on porches during working hours, or Mexican "Lo-Riders" wearing dark hats and holding huge knives. He has never met any poor people, Russians, or Iranians. He hasn't read anything about them at all. He avoids ALL poor people. He just knows they want all the stuff he's bought and they want him to be as poor as they are. His mind might secretly harbor the idea that it would be better to go ahead and kill off everybody that doesn't agree with him and the world would be a better place. With the money he has spent on "protection" he could very easily have taken vacations or done a few things he enjoyed. But he has wasted what little time he will be on this earth staying hidden away in his pitiful little house that's all wired up to tell him when a "boogey man" is trying to break in.

Let's face it, if a burglar wants to break into your house, he will do it. An alarm won't stop him and if he's a professional, he'll get around booby traps and harmful items. Most of us realize that the real purpose of an alarm system is to allow us some peace of mind while we're at the movies. A $100 system will do just about as much as a $1000 unit.

Just after the Depression, a large part of our money went to public works projects that had the people who had been pawns in the power struggle building dams, parks, public buildings, high school stadiums in order to make a living. The problem with this idea, according to some, was the fact that it supposedly took away a man's drive and made him depend on "handouts." I think the real reason some disapprove was that parks didn't benefit the investor class and there was no way for them to make money because it went to people who didn't invest in areas the high finance people liked, such as real estate, banking, insurance, and stock. Defense, on the other hand, puts money in the pockets of people who will continue to use it (rather than live on it) for the betterment of those in finance. Better yet, items for defense will decay and will need to be replaced, like the concept of light bulbs that only have a few hours of life (Could they easily build a bulb that would burn forever?)

Another great concept concerning defense is the fact it's the government's way of rewarding states that follow their policies. It's no happenstance that many states, such as Texas, are getting so much of the defense dollars these days because they are possibly so important to fostering the current administration's political stand. In the days of the pyramids, the rulers used slave labor and paid them a meager wage, or nothing at all. The materials used generated the economy and the stone merchant, rope merchant, etc., made money that kept them from revolting against the government. NO SPACE CADETS! ★

Do you ever get tired of hearing about how well criminals are doing? How much cocaine dealers make, or how some doo-dah union leader gets away

with stealing from the pension fund? I do, I hate it! I do my little jobs, collect my stupid little checks and pay all my pitiful bills. I give money to IRS, which I really don't mind, and whatever is left, I play with. The concept of buying a yacht or a penthouse in Miami is beyond my scope. I get excited when I buy a first edition of a George Orwell, which costs about as much as a gram of coke, but will do nothing more than make me aware of all my root canals and won't give me $200 boogers.

Why do these people get rewarded? What's wrong with this goofy society where we admire some creep who gets away with murder, drug deals, or even a hostile takeover of a corporation? NO GETTING AWAY WITH IT!

We'll all pile into a car to go see a movie about some creep who comes from Cuba and becomes a hit man or gangster while we wouldn't pay a nickel to see a movie about a woman who works two jobs to send her kid to college, while

she suffers from a pinched nerve, bad hip, and loss of youthful appearance. I think the TV show "Miami Vice" is nothing more than a fast version of "Lives of the Rich and Famous"... a fashion cop movie where, I think, people actually root for the drug dealers because they have such great houses and cars. I hate 'em! NO REWARDS!

Every time I go into a spaghetti joint, I wonder if it's a money laundry for some Mafia slime's profit from whores. Olive oil supports gun deals and pizza pays for hit men and car bombs. I'm becoming a paranoid fool! It drives me crazy to think of people getting away with it while I sit over here hacking and hewing out money for frozen dinners and an occasional pint of Butter Pecan ice cream. Damn those guys! I dislike seeing them glorified, admired, and, especially, winning.

Making money is easy. All you have to do is give people what they want or that which they can't get easily. Drugs, guns, cheap deals on stolen merchandise, dirty movies, hookers, gambling, horse racing... immoral money stuff. Doesn't anybody work anymore? NO WORK!

In a society that respects wealth and accumulation more than integrity, it's easy to see the fascination with those who get rich quick, any way they can. There are people who relish a cheap stereo even if they suspect it was stolen. They chuckle when they imply it may be "hot." There is a certain grin on the faces of those who win in Las Vegas or on a football pool, the grin of greed. It's the same look that many corporate types get when they crush a competitor and drive him out of business. A good number of people respect the swiftness of justice found among the Mafia. You don't play the game and you're dead. Well, I hate the "game" and I don't care for those who play it... legal or illegal. I'm proud of not being a good "player" when it comes to running over other people who do what I do.

Let's get mad about low rent criminals! Let's not buy books about their lives or pay to see movies that give them a shred of credibility. Boo, criminals! Ca Ca! Get away, get away! I love to rant and rave. ★

I've often wondered how we can so easily hand over the power of saying NO. We grant others authority over our lives like a prisoner who hand picks the jailer that will keep him locked up in a custom designed cell. Is he keeping himself locked in or the world locked out? Ask Paul Fussell.

When we give up our right of free choice to somebody who has, incidentally,

proclaimed their ability for such a job we are actually saying, "Please tell us NO so we won't have to assume responsibility for our own actions." We use our tax dollars to pay a government to tell us NO although we'd often just rather keep the money. They tell us NO to a business lunch when we know that meeting with a client's stupid brother in the siding business could be the difference between buying new office furniture or having to moonlight.

We pay preachers to tell us NO when it comes to doing things our natural instincts say YES about. NO SLEEPING LATE ON SUNDAY, NO KEEPING THAT EXTRA 10%, NO CHOOSING THE BEST FROM ALL FAITHS, NO USING OUR LOGIC and certainly NO PUTTING OUR FAITH IN OUR FELLOW MAN. In my mind, the ultimate NO sign is that which says, MAN WAS BORN NO GOOD, he hits the floor a sinner, this according to the preacher who puts his understanding of righteousness above our own and parks his Cadillac in the driveway of a tax-free house in the meantime. NO PARKING! ★

Thanks to computers and mailing lists, we are being flooded with charismatic messages direct from the Supreme Deity. Messages that promise instant wealth and riches, like a celestial Dale Carnegie course. Surely, with so much input and handling by typesetters, printers and such, those messages are bound to occasionally get scrambled. How do we say NO to information that is proven to be wrong or, at least, exists in a giant grey area like: Sex education encourages teenagers to engage in premarital sex, while sexual ignorance doesn't.

I wish that people like Jerry Falwell, Pat Robertson, Jimmy Swaggart, and the others would occasionally say NO to overloads of self-righteousness and the ability to interpret the Bible better than anyone else. Just because you can hold a congregation of like-minded people in the palm of your hand doesn't automatically give you full knowledge in all worldly matters such as politics, literature, and social needs... particularly in a democratic country such as America where the majority doesn't usually agree with extremism. Power is a funny thing, it's hard to say NO to because it's usually backed up with a certain amount of financial success. People suddenly listen to Willie Nelson, Mick Jagger, professional football players, and people like Mr. Falwell, all of whom believe their own press and often speak in areas of which they are often ignorant... South Africa is a good example. I'm reminded of a wonderful Irish quote. "There is nothing so passionate as vested interest disguised as moral conviction." ★

Let's pretend that a chemical plant on the west coast goes amuck and spills out tons of toxins that only affect children between 12 and 20 years of age. This group would suddenly begin eating their fingers, drinking Drano, and collecting bag worms. Would we see a "Teen Movie" showing the funny side of this disorder? I think we would... I think we do!

Is there anything that movie producers will simply ignore? Do we have to play up every stupid malfunction of our youth just because a bunch of people will pay to see it? Good grief! There are people who would pay big money to see films of executions. Will nobody gamble on a film

> No performances between the half-hour and the hour.

that shows kids for what they are... simple, new people on the road to discovery, who don't know zip about life? Must every kid be a computer whiz, great karate fighter, junior scientist, super stud, or fool who can't cut it with the opposite sex? Must we always have the nerd against the social wonders, football team, thugs, or R.O.T.C.? NO BEACH BLANKET BINGO!

I wonder why we rarely see sensible sex in teen movies. Sex where they use contraceptives and don't speak of marriage…like real life. One factor in the downfall of teen movies are the censors and investors…two groups with a misplaced perspective on life. One wants to control the world through denial and the other wants to control the world through financial power. They will both omit reality in movies because of the box office. "We can show the chick getting hacked to death with a chain saw, but the part where she enjoys good sex with the kid has got to go," we might hear. If a girl takes off her clothes in the early part of the flick she's in for it. Bad girls attract sharks, ax murderers, and people returning from the dead.

While we push morality in teen shows, we can see a double standard in other areas of society. Scantily clad girls on film is a negative and scantily clad girls in a beauty contest is a positive. Girls can't show their underwear on the one hand, but it's perfectly okay when it's a cheerleader or majorette. "Nothing suggestive," we hear. Don't they realize that a tree fork can be suggestive to a teenage boy? He'll hump a pump-

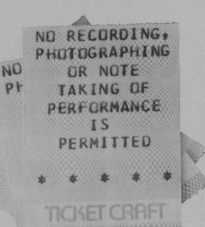

kin or a foam rubber pillow if he gets a chance. Let's be real! NO FALSIES!

There are films and there are movies. One is a potential piece of art while the other is pure entertainment. What would happen if we began to see more films for teenagers and fewer movies? What if we actually addressed problems or ideas that were real rather than exaggerated stereotypes? If we give teens credit for having sense maybe they would let us see more of it. NO CREDIT!

The same thing is happening to movies that has been happening to literature: business first, art last. "A Thousand Clowns," "The Last Picture Show," and "My Bodyguard" were close to teen art, while "Friday the 13th" and "I-X" are not.

Don't get me wrong. I know we need a certain amount of mindless, shallow, base, naive, simplistic, and meaningless pap for teens to sit and stuff themselves with junk from the concession counter. I just wish that we would see more "Breaking Away" type films than "Porky's." ★

People who said NO to movie roles:
Grace Kelly to CAT ON A HOT TIN ROOF
Rod Steiger to PATTON
Buddy Ebsen to TIN MAN in WIZARD OF OZ
W. C. Fields to WIZARD in WIZARD OF OZ
Ronald Reagan to CASABLANCA
Gregory Peck to AFRICAN QUEEN

There is something tragically wrong with a society that will pay two men hundreds of thousands of dollars to beat each other unconscious, bloody each other's noses, or split eyebrows. There is also a serious malfunction in a world that will revere such people as boxers, while they seldom have the same praise for doctors, teachers, or scientists. We will probably never go to an event where there are slides showing lethal infectious bacteria being K.O.'ed by new drugs. We'll not buy ringside seats to a debate where scientists attack the process of aging. "Keep it simple, stupid," as our brainy friends in the service like to say. NO PUNCHES!

Boxing is the lowest form of spectator sport, right down there with bearbaiting, cock fights, dog fights, or putting two male cats in a burlap bag. That it gets any attention whatsoever is astounding. The fact is: Professional fights would probably die a fast death if the stakes weren't so high. It's not the fight that churns people as much as the fact they'll be getting a fortune. Poor people love fights because it's something they conceivably could do...much the way the middle class feels about golf and tennis. It's every kid's dream of escape from the ghetto by using his fists...a cheap tool. He sure isn't going to get out by becoming a banker, lawyer, or doctor. Through boxing he can get neighborhood respect, some money, and a couple of chicks who also want to be special by association. He can be somebody until his brain cells have been killed off and he ends up as a fry cook named "Champ."

I don't fault boxers; they obviously don't know any better. I fault the slimedog promoter who would make money promoting public amputations or cat drownings if he thought it would bring in a crowd. Promoting is the downside of the free enterprise system. It has every "Joe Bob" in the country trying to find a way of making a quick buck off of some poor fool who'll take a chance by endangering his life. NO CHANCE!

If it's a matter of supply and demand, then I feel that those on the demand side should have to fight one another for tickets in front of the arena...the strongest gets ringside while the weaker gets balcony. Survival of the fittest...isn't that what it's all about? ★

The word NO can be so tragically final. When uttered by Sister Assumption the word could mean: "Infraction will lead directly to eternal hellfire, suffering, and pain without the benefit of Sainthood or a seat at the bingo table." When the word came from Jennie Beth Stanfield during a spectacular one-finger bra clasp flip, it meant: "You will not touch the lily white skin of a female until it's the arm of a nurse adjusting your plasma valve on your 70th birthday"... even though that flesh had been handled by every guy on the "A" football team, including Wesley DeFord, who had pimples as big as parakeets. I think NO was invented as a foreplay term.

Most of the girls I knew as a young race-horse had learned to manipulate the word NO by the age of four. Not viciously or evilly, just power-fully. In a world of crossed signals, they seemed to have me wondering if NO meant YES, or vice versa, with a simple eye flutter or a shoulder slink. I've done the dumbest things in my life try-ing to get the right grin to follow the emphatic NO or to avoid that same facile expression in her eyes after a solid YES. I've driven my car fast, walked with a slouch, and maintained a constant sneer in hope of foiling those terrible signals, only to end up staring in the mirror, a crushed human, wondering why I had played such a fool.

I've often wondered if mothers and daughters practice "Manmanship" while on shopping tours or strolls through malls. In my mind I can see the most respectable mom (like Beaver Cleaver's mother) talking to her young

charge: "You want to bring him to the point of a babbling fool, then look him straight in the eye, with a glare tell him NO...wait five seconds, then give a number two giggle and say, 'You're cute when you're mad!'"

Could it be that the whole premise of slumber parties is actually some type of NO boot camp where participants learn "verbal karate" and the mystic use of NO... maybe they dress as boys so their sisters in training can practice various foils and putdowns.

I think the use of NO for women ranks right along with the secrets of how to make dresses ride up thighs without using hands, seductive hair flips, shoulder drops, and that wiggle with their lower extremities that they never do unless men are around.

Luckily for humanity, women control sex, which controls the gene pool that moves our species forward. Their job is to pick a mate that best reflects their genetic and physiological makeup that will guarantee offspring that don't have eyes like a weimaraner, a missing chin, or excessive nosebleeds... like when rich people marry their cousins. If this job were left up to men, who knows what would happen to our species. The woman picks the man and I think women may actually be the superior of our species and deserve the power of NO.

To get around "the power," and survive, a man must learn women's signals when using NO. When you ask a woman who is a potential lover to do something and she quickly says, "Sure!" you must do a double check. If her eyes dart away or she immediately notices a hangnail, it's a NO for sure. Or when you say you have a friend that has a lake cabin and would she care to go, listen to mentionings of shopping for a swimsuit or a discussion of groceries and tanning oil to be sure she really meant YES.

Yet, women have similar problems reading men. If a man swears up and down that NO, he isn't just trying for the "bad thing," and YES he would be happy to maintain a simple friendship...women, watch men's eyes to see where they're staring during the conversation. That's why guys love to wear sunglasses. NO GLASS! ★

It's often been said that men give love to get sex and women give sex to get love. These sexual politics reflect the ultimate NO. So many of our social and moral laws are concerned with sex that all things are touched. War is possibly a way to gain more power for men to attract or capture women. Our defense system is aimed at protecting our families, which translates to women and children...not that women need protecting, for they have been proven to be vicious fighters and strong competitors in all areas of the so-called "man's world."

As for NO concerning first sex, the olden, golden days of the Middle East supplied a ton of rules directed at the subject of who could do what to whom...nearly always in a man's favor. Adultery, for instance, was made a NO-NO because a man could force himself on a "maiden," whether she agreed or not. If he was successful in changing the maiden status, she would be compelled to marry him if he so chose...which he often did because he became her legal guardian and keeper of the keys to her wealth and property. This made for an easy stepping-stone into wealthier circles. What was worse was the fact that a man from another clan or tribe could get access to the wealth of the maiden's clan or tribe, particularly if the maiden was of royal lineage. The rule against fooling around was quickly added to the tribal law books, mostly for economic reasons, certainly not for the welfare of the maiden, who was a necessary evil in the process of continuing heritage. The wealthy of today still have pretty strong rules concerning who their daughters say YES to. Some are taught early that one must say NO to those fellows without proper respect for "The Club," that includes marital/financial mergers, social and political parity, or at least a strong respect for those important pre-wedding functions that give both families a chance to compare assets. I often wonder if spoiling their young isn't, in reality, a way to assure the constant need for the "good life" that will guarantee a firm NO when confronted by those suitors from a lower station. Could a finishing school, besides being a place to learn the art of whipping out a game hen dinner on the

spur of the moment, actually be a training base
designed to break the least bit of rebellion that
would put emotion over economics? NO SLUMMING! ★

I will never understand why I'm so completely lucky. The world of new found fortune seems to be knocking on my door weekly. In the last few days I have won a chance at a free outboard motor boat, a mobile home with all the trimmings, an

RCA color TV enclosed in a home entertainment unit or a miniature grandfather clock...which do you think I'll win if I visit Pecan Hills Estates? I also received a non-negotiable check for One Million Dollars and a personal note from Johnny Carson's sidekick (I didn't even know he liked me). My mail is a daily adventure featuring wonderful surprises and "deals." My soul is happy because of all the "religibiz" preachers who spend hours a day praying for me or want to send me a Miracle Cross, Last Supper Table Cloth, or Blessed Olive Oil from the trees around Calvary...for nothing more than a mere "Love Offering" ($100, $50, $25 or Other...check one). NO SALE!

The tricks these turkeys use to get your attention, or at least avoid the trash can, are very innovative. Replicas of Treasury checks, IRS envelopes, fake telegrams, false notifications of winning, and total fabrications are printed on the outside of the piece. Window envelopes that show your name printed on check paper are the best, especially when used in conjunction with a patriotic stamp meter seal or a message that reads: Buy US Savings Bonds!

Don't these fools realize that the effect is lost when you get three a day? Of course they've probably done studies on the mental level of their target markets and they've learned to "Sparkle" the bribe in accordance with the "glitter level" of the audience. Early traders used the same technique with natives who would sign over their land for a string of beads, shiny knives, or a mirror. These people know that a family of Flatheads will actually drive out to some piece of scrubgrass-bespeckled land next to a dammed-up creek (usually called something like Hidden Lake or Rainbow Falls) on the weekend just to get a set of $9.95 cookware (valued at $69). The poor people usually say: "Well, Verona, it'll be a nice drive and we can act like we're interested and get some free food...ain't no sumbitch gonna sell me sumthin' I don't want!" In the weeks that follow they'll be telling their friends: "Hell, we were surprised! That land will be worth five times as much money when they get the water and electricity out there... when the lake gets full it'll be 20 feet from our sun deck. We bought two lots so we can sell one later!" Right. NO LOITERING ON THE BEACH!

The saddest thing about junk mail is its waste. I look at a week's worth of mail, a pretty good pile, and I think of all the people who got the same amount, which they throw in the trash as well. I think of the trees that were totally wasted so some zealot speculator can get a shot at pawning off sheet metal spice jars, crummy ball-point pens, or steak knives...gambling on percentages like a net fisherman. NO FISHING!

I wish that the post office would simply take the mail cost up a few clicks for commercial lures and put the mail hyenas on the run. If a company has something that's of true value, they won't mind the price as much and the cost will be built into the price of the item. Religious mail

should be priced three times as high or it should
be dropped from airplanes so angels can direct it
into the right homes...Celestial Air Mail.
NO STAMPS! ★

I listen in wonder at the amount of NO signals connected with the "bad thing"... sex. We hear a silent, but boastful YES when it comes to being a workaholic, a material bore, a religious zealot; a Type A overachiever with high blood pressure; a golf freak who ignores his family; an ultra-careerist who lets his or her lover slide away; or a sexist... but let a reference to good sex, women's rights in the bedroom, or pure sexual freedom slip out and you hear NO echoing off every wall. When a child asks questions or touches himself "down there," out pops an emphatic NO. If they want to see a friend undressed, they hear NO while they'll hear a strong YES when it comes to defending some minor ego problem with a fist fight. "We don't run, son!"

I asked somebody the other day: "You'd keep your child from seeing a movie that showed a woman's breast, much like the one he grew up on, while you'd let him see "Rambo" with all its torture, gore, and killing?" The reply was "Damn right!" Sick, I say.

Our problem with sex being a NO-NO might come from our old friend, St. Paul (who was said to be a little misguided in the area, so misguided, in fact, that he is rumored to have castrated himself or at least mutilated his man-hood to the point of non-functioning). He was not just against sex out of wedlock, he was against any sex whatsoever, a custom said to be practiced by the Essene and Qumran sects of ancient times (150 B.C.), the possible foundation of modern Christianity. Celibacy for religious reasons may stem from the fact that our contact with Adam and Eve, and therefore, original sin, is continued by procreation as a result of sex and lust. If we all stopped fooling around, original sin would be stopped in its tracks and the human race would die... allowing purity in the next life. Therefore, sex is a big NO according to St. Paul, and women fared no better: "... it is good for a man not to touch a woman," he proposed that men COULD take a wife, "to avoid fornication." This was a grudging concession, given "by permission, and not of commandment. For I would that all men were even as I myself" (1 Corinthians 7:7).

What's our problem with sexuality? Most of us don't have a snapshot of our naked body. It's okay to pull our clothes off to save our lives in the middle of a freeway after an accident but... take NO pictures.

Speaking of nudism, I don't think naked bodies are really pornographic anymore. Most of our youth would rather see a body with a thousand dollars worth of clothes on it. Fashion catalogs are the new pornography. NO MINORS!

I don't know how we ever make it in life. It's like a salmon swimming up river, cutting himself to pieces, just to spawn. We are jerked from a warm womb into the cold as we get our bottoms spanked, penises cut (no wonder we think of them so much), and then are taken from our mothers, later to get a cold nipple, then a return to a lonely nursery. You may say NO to the world in the first five minutes. NO WAITING! ★

I've always felt that working for somebody was a type of personal contract. You pay me a certain amount and I work in your interest for a pre-determined amount of time. That's the basis of hourly wages. Every construction worker or factory type knows this. They are paid so much per hour based on so many hours per week...the 40 hour week is a popular term we often hear. Now we are hearing about a giant separation of working terms that describe our position: Tradesman, laborer, sales, clerical, and now, the mysterious professional. The difference between professional and the other four is the fact that professionals have NO hours...they are expected to work as long as the job takes and their salary is based on a monthly wage. This stinks. Most professionals, such as engineers, architects, stock brokers and such, perform services that are billed out by the company on an hourly basis. If an engineer is paid X dollars for an approximate 40 hour week, he is expected to work towards producing 40 billable hours in order to earn his pay. If he works an additional 20 hours a week in order to complete a job, he bills 60 hours to the client. The company gets 20 free hours of profit. NO DEAL!

One of the sickest terms in the business world is: "We expect 110% from our people." There is no such thing as 110%, especially when the company doesn't expect to pay 110% for the extra effort. NO PERCENTAGE!

Another great mystery in the corporate world is the "pecking order" that is used to get that 110%. Use of the corporate lunchroom, washroom, covered parking, or club memberships is a shallow bribe...even a damned window is used by some as a carrot for getting a person to give more than he's paid for. NO CARROTS!

An amusing tradition is that of wood wall-paneling. The president gets his office panelled to the ceiling while the vice president gets paneling only halfway up the wall and the junior V.P. gets the old furniture from the two top guys, or an office with a window. Important stuff, boys.

Have you ever noticed that the most boring men in a corporation always seem to be the guys who have to give speeches at the convention or sales meetings? On top of that, they usually have a clever, professional writer to write their speeches! I think everyone should be required to write their own speeches so the world can see how boring they actually are...at least they should give credit to the actual writer. This should also apply to our President...in fact, if we like what he's saying so much, maybe we should elect the speech writer. NO TALKING!

Corporate identity has become a religion with the company Godhead and his closest apostles, operating in a heavenly chapel on the top floor, where those who actually do their bidding would fail to comprehend the mysteries. The company bible sets the rules on who shall live and who shall leave, if the commandments aren't followed. The rules of the religion were written hundreds of years ago by men who felt they weren't responsible to the people, but for the people. Men who felt a democratic method of doing business would lead to the loss of power as the ignorant and dull-minded masses gained the right to determine direction they had no knowledge of. How could they, without the proper schooling and acquired respect for "the way things are done." NO TICKEE, NO WASHEE!

NO TICKEE... NO SHIRTEE!

People are often SO amazed when a giant corporation gets in trouble or goes broke. All you need to do is visit a corporate office and see the ceramic dolphins, sheet metal sculpture, golf awards, and bent horseshoe nail sculpture of a little golfer or skiier to see where the "Big Gun's" thought processes come from... see one of them on the golf course in lime green golf pants with a silly little hat with a fuzzy ball on top for a burst of reality. NO BALLS! ★

Somewhere in the back of my mind there exists a little voice that says NO every time my confidence seems to be getting strong. One second I have this small electrical shiver that runs between my shoulder blades... As it connects, my mind says: "Well, things are going pretty good now and there's no reason to believe that they won't continue." Then the voice cries: "NO! This is just a temporary high and if you allow yourself to drop your guard you'll get crunched twice as bad!" That same voice often says: "NO, you're not special," "NO, she's not interested in you," "NO, you'll never be a success." Sometimes it shows its ugly head in the form of "Can't," "Shouldn't," or "Forget it." I don't know why this negative rascal is always ready to slip in some mental judo.

Somehow the image of NO gives us comfort and a reason not to try, while the scary "Possible," or the potentially disappointing YES would leave rumbling quakes in the backs of our minds... like wishing for that special Christmas present. If you were told NO to a present, it would certainly send you into temporary fits that would soon subside. Whereas, the statement, "We'll see" or "Maybe" would drive you crazy. "Expect the worst while you hope for the best." The effect marginally destroys the "best" even if it comes to be... if you get a bike or a special doll, you might be mad at the toy and the giver because they had caused you so much turmoil, of which the end was only an anticlimax..."Big Deal." NO FALSE EXPECTATIONS! ★

I'm really not much of a spectator. The idea of sitting through four quarters of basketball, football, or hockey hits me pretty much like spending a day at my late Aunt Maude's house, where the major activity was recounting her collection of ceramic poodles or building numerous card houses with my Uncle Beecher's Shriner Cards. I know that the people on the field or court are having a better time than I. I'm not capable of building myself to a fever pitch over some retired music teacher's continuous version of "Bolero," "Granada," or the "Charge Call." Personally, I think they should just play the last quarter, since it's always the most exciting. That way they could have four games a night and the season would be over in one week.

The only thing worse than sports is media "Sportstalk" where some over-the-hill has-been wallows in the efforts of younger people who still have the physical ability to run into each other because their young bones mend so easily. The main purpose of sports shows is to fill time and give event results so those that gamble on sports can either pay up or get money. NO SPORTS TALK UNLESS YOU PLAY!

I don't look back at my high school days and wish I could return. They weren't the happiest days of my life. However, I can look back and see that the people I disliked in school are, pretty much, the same people I dislike today. The guy who told the coach that I was out late with a girl is now with the State Tax department. The guy who turned me in for not wearing my R.O.T.C. uniform off campus got his head blown off while doing something stupid in Viet Nam. The top runner, who always hounded me about running harder, now hounds me about insurance...now that I think about it, most of the top athletes are now pushing insurance. Sports are the backbone of sales because it always offers a base for small talk — the mule of marketing.

While we're on sports, I noticed an interesting thing. Certain events attract certain people...i.e., wrestling, car races, and bowling attract more fat people, while basketball, tennis and polo seem to attract more skinny people. Football, hockey, and soccer seem to appeal to both fat and skinny people. The events for more wealthy folks (country club sports like golf and tennis) are more fashionable and don't really include the public. Basketball has more guys dressed in suits while wrestling has more people dressed in T-shirts. One sees more people wearing hats indoors at tractor pulls, dirt bike races, and rodeos. Baseball has NO class system.

In ancient Rome, the powers-that-were felt they could keep the poor from revolt with a series of circuses and free bread. All week people looked forward to the shows and free eats, much the same as we look forward to the Super Bowl, while the rulers continued on courses that would lead to the fall of the Empire. I often think about the sporting scores on the day we bombed Libya and attacked Grenada. ★

According to those in the know, fashion ranks right along there with the proper fork or soup spoon, in the social order of things. Frankly, I'm mystified about who says YES and NO when it comes to fashion. When I think of fashion, I'm reminded of Nehru jackets and mood rings. How can anybody laugh at a mini-skirt when it was obviously so important in its time. I mean, one simply can't pick and choose what one finds fashionable. If it's in "Cosmo," "Vogue," or "Bazaar" it must be right. Who are we to say that a garment like the "middie" or sack dress was wrong? What about gold lame, which we see in all the "better" bath and lingerie shops? It's elegant? Elegant is a great word. It's used most by merchants and hookers (probably for the same reason). I just can't figure out who chose to use it first, strippers or the Junior League.

How does fashion happen? My guess is that somewhere (probably New York) somebody is sitting behind a very expensive desk looking at fabric and patterns while they scream, in a shrill voice, "Gawd No, Berry. This has to go... it's so pedestrian!" If a garment color or look is so totally important now that to be without it is to fall from social grace and a fait par erreur, then why will it be a disaster next year? Because clothes manufacturers won't make any money off new stuff, is my guess. Fashion is fun, isn't it?

Something occurred to me the other day while watching a Love Boat rerun. Fashion freaks rarely say NO to anything that appears in late-night TV movies or in old "Life" or "Collier's" magazines. You'll notice that we never see a

revival of clothes from the 1800's. It's because we know that movies on that subject feature only costumes while Fred Astaire, Cary Grant, and "The Thin Man" wore everyday stuff; expensive stuff that we can still buy in used clothes stores when we want to look spiffy at a gallery opening. Fred, Cary, David, and Monty all had it. We're all grownups here, so we can speak of "gay" influence without hollering "prejudice!" My theory is that the new men's look, for each fashion period, is developed first and the women's look is designed to complement it, rather than the other way around. If the new men's look is going to be "pre-War German," "English Finishing School," or "1940 Boys at the Beach," then the new women's look will agree with it, as will their hair styles, shoes, and accessories. The last round of "new/old" designers were enthralled with James Dean, Monty Clift, and Tyrone Power (for obvious reasons) from the 50's. Hence, we have a heavy fifties image. Since time didn't change very fast in those days, it has carried over into a 60's look as well... not quite beyond the baby boom designer's memory.

If America wants to get the edge on the NO word in fashion anytime soon, I suggest some simple speculation: 1. Late night TV will soon be flooded with old "hippie" movies because that segment of the baby boom will want to wallow in the past; 2. Hippies

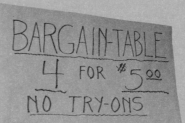

used a lot of costly fabric (retreads that they were) like satin, denim, silk, and leather...all the natural stuff which will fit in nicely; 3. There are bound to be some fashion role models (men) that appeal to current designer's taste like Peter Fonda, Roger Daltry, or Tiny Tim; 4. Bell bottoms, denim skirts, marching jackets, and "the layer look" all required a lot of material which can run up the price; 5. There were scads of accessories, like beads, headbands, scarves, weird footwear, silly hats, and dumb glasses which will profit the accessory market... a group that deserves a turn. All these things are probably still in a warehouse somewhere... already written off as a loss! This means cheap: an American look in an American price structure!

My suggestion is that we get together some primo examples of Hippie clothes, put them on some models who look really bored and stand them in front of the Eiffel Tower and shoot a couple of pictures of them in contorted and tortured poses and send them back to America on a wire or TV cable that can be shown at "The Market." Since they appear to be French, orders would pour into France...which they cannot produce. American makers would suddenly show up with all the leftovers of the 60's and "Ta da!" We win and say NO to French control in the process. Of course this will be an uphill fight because everybody likes the tax writeoffs on trips to France and Europe...and the French like to come here and scoff.

What's the deal with France? Have you noticed that the big fashion NO words are French? Just because they did a big silk trade in olden times, they should control the world? Are there no good designers in Lapland, Norway, or Israel? I would wonder, with all the Jewish power in the rag business, why Israel isn't the capital so they can deal with somebody who speaks the language.

Of course we all know that France has some of the oldest manufacturers around and they've called the shots for years. They also rarely say NO to anything they have designed. They keep the edge. They know that American rag makers, in our great free enterprise tradition, will "knock-off" the French look with cheap imitations. Thus, the only way they can put a stop to this process is to proclaim the "Look" null and void, usually about the time it hits Sear's or J.C. Penney's.

Fashion is another example of how we so easily give up our rights by letting somebody we don't know tell us NO when it comes to dressing  the way we like. The only way polyester would ever become fashionable would be for manufacturers to pull it completely off the market and reintroduce it at $50 a yard. I use polyester only as an example of a fashion trend gone bad that was loved by many because it stretched around their chubby little bottoms and made them think they were wearing a size smaller.

I say people should be allowed to wear what makes them comfortable rather than being told NO by people who make more money on new looks, colors, or fabrics. Right away, I'm sure the mental switchboards are lit up! "The public controls fashion and the rag merchants simply meet that demand," I will hear. I'm sure the failure of the "middie" look will be cited. Balderdash, I say! If you go into a store that is current, you will only find fashion which is current. If the public actually had the power to say NO most women would still buy MuMu dresses and Raja shoes... comfortable garments that were loved by suburbia. Fat women would say NO to those stupid and dangerous pointed shoes and men would gladly hang tie manufacturers. If the public controlled fashion, people would wear sweat shirts and tennis shoes to work. More importantly, only fools would spend hundreds of dollars to get an outfit that looked just like that of another. I'm still amused when ten guys show up in a room wearing blue blazers, tan pants, light blue shirts with regimental ties, and Oxford loafers, having responded to fashion copy that reads: "An image as totally unique as you are." NO COPYING! ★

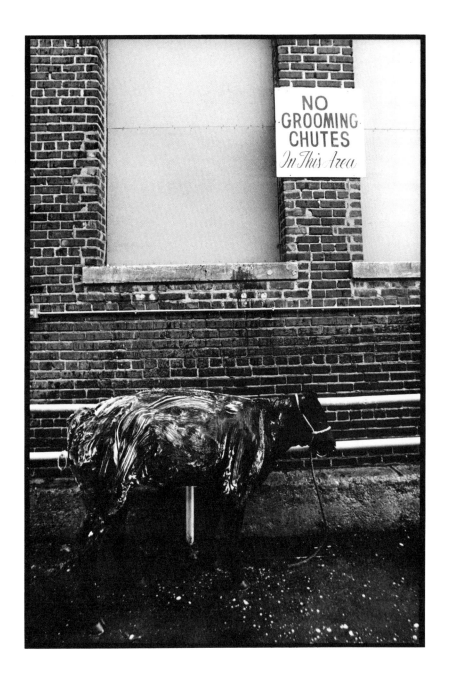

We are not perfect. None of us. The President, the Pope, Miss America, your Mom, Brooke Shields, or even Jerry Falwell, all have hidden mannerisms they hope the world never knows. We all do certain things that are cultural or social taboos, like picking our teeth with an insurance man's business card or listening to others' conversations. NO SHAME!

I say come out of our closets with our weird habits. No more secret guilt or self-degradation when we:

Act like we're taking down a phone number of somebody we don't like, who is on the other end;

Use double the amount of toilet paper in a public rest room;

Eat candy bars in the car when we're on a diet... so people won't see;

Move our mouths to hymns when we don't know the words;

Bow our heads and not really pray at sporting events;

Park in spaces for the handicapped and walk with a limp;

Buy quarts of ice cream and tell the clerk we're buying it for a party of 10;

Look down women's blouses or up their dresses;

Sniff our armpits or fingers;

Wear different color socks when wearing boots;

Watch dogs, squirrels, and birds performing sex;

Pick pimples when next to a mirror;

Get up before our new lover, to put on makeup so he won't see;

Stuff before a date, then eat like a bird;

Look at people's checkbooks when they go out of the room;

Go through people's medicine cabinets when we visit;

Lift our chest when in the presence of the opposite sex;

Lie about our income to telephone researchers or on questionnaires;

Clean up the apartment before the maid comes... so she won't see how bad we are;

Lie about an appointment time when on a family outing with mom;

Follow fire trucks and ambulances;

Go into a place alone and act as if we're meeting someone by looking around;

Lie on job resumes;

Keep the extra money when the bank teller screws up;

Call lovers to see if they're home, and then hang up;

Send an anonymous erotic note to our lover to see if they respond to us;

Tell people we have an exotic heritage; i.e., "I'm one-quarter Cherokee";

Make a minor operation into a life threatening experience;

Speak of a large family inheritance that will never exist;

Lie about our sexual experiences...or VD history;

Buy evening dresses and return them after a social event to get money back;

Blow smoke in the face of a friend's pet to make it go away;

Make out utility checks wrong when we don't have the money so they will be returned;

Put the right payment date on a late payment check;

Use traffic as an excuse for tardiness;

Don't tell a friend that their lover is ugly or cheating;

Tell people that their children are beautiful when we don't mean it;

Intentionally guess people's ages lower than what's obvious;

Say a crummy haircut looks good;

Wear underwear longer than what's safe;

Wear a hat or scarf when our hair is dirty;

Run the water in the rest room so people will think we've washed our hands after doing our business;

Use the nearest curtain to get rid of sweat when people are out of the room;

Put gum on the bottom of chairs;

Eat leftovers off people's plates in the kitchen;

Get triple portions of food at a buffet and pick up two forks as if we're going to share;

Walk by the swimming pool and act like we're looking for a friend in order to see bikiniettes;

Stand near a dressing room with a curtain to try to see through the opening;

Look through the feminine hygiene and contraceptive section to see what's new.

We do weird things. We're human and there are really no rules about life. Let's accept our weirdness and realize that we are okay...it just doesn't matter. ★

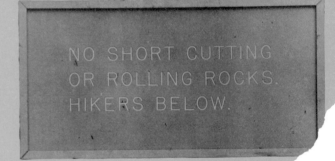

What has happened to free enterprise? The way it was taught to me by the grossly idealistic Mrs. VanValkenburg, was: through competition, companies and manufacturers worked to make us happy on the supply and demand theory. A good product got a public YES while a poor product got a resounding NO. We controlled the NO and they were supposed to work hard for the YES. A better mousetrap and all that "path to your door" jazz. Fine.

But then something happened. Products began to come apart in our hands, yet the makers said: "Phooey." We said YES to Mr. Orlando's drug store and it went under, only to be replaced by Super Bee Drugs where we had to take a number after we walked through the shoplifting guards or where a teenage kid behind the counter would holler out, "What kinda rubbers you want?" We said YES to Hank's Atomic Gas Station, Wally's Hollywood Shoes, the Food Basket Grocery, Talk O' The Town Cafe, Wexler's Dairy, and Pepe's Auto-motive. They all went under, only to be replaced by Sello Gas at a buck-seventy nine a gallon (Hank charged 38¢), Shoeworld, Skaggs Grocery/ Dime Store/Drugs/Hardware and Video Bar, Milkmaster's Nuway Chemojuice, and Danny Dealer's Automotive where they repair your car by replacing everything until the noise stops. We said NO to most of these joints and they laughed and said: "Who cares, there's plenty more where you come from." They are the only game in town. We mutter NO under our breath while we make out a check for a tuneup that would have been a month's salary in the old days and damned if they don't make you wait while they call the bank to see if it's good!

The power of the NO word has been lost to consumers. NO HELPFULNESS, NO FOLLOW THROUGH, NO INFORMATION ON PRODUCTS, NO SPECIAL ATTENTION and other NO words (stated or silent) have replaced the old. We don't get to pick and choose; we get to pump our own gas, fill our own bags, weigh our own produce, and then are required to have the correct change.

Did you ever try to say NO to a utility company? Don't try it in times of extreme heat or cold. Not only do you have to say YES to any amount they want to charge, but you had better pay it on the correct day or you'll get a finance charge. I wish I could do that! You want to holler NO at something? Say, NO GAS COMPANY, PHONE COMPANY, OR ELECTRIC COMPANY ADVERTISING. Why do they need to promote? Why do they need color brochures and those dumb recipes that come in some of our monthly bills? I can't afford to make Capt'n Willy's Hawaiian Wonder Chicken because I'm eating Bob's Ranch Beans because I'm broke because of utility bills! NO BILLS! ★

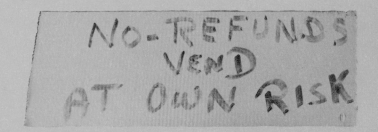

There are situations in our society where the silent NO sign exists. Like a snake eating its own tail, these unsaid policies consume national morality. While they offer one message on the front side, there is an opposite message on the other. Many would quickly read the front with pride, with no regard for its opposite, double-edged meaning, like a negative Yin and Yang.

NO WELFARE & NO FREE JOB TRAINING

NO SPEEDING & NO FINES FOR RADAR DETECTORS

NO LOITERING & NO PUBLIC YOUTH CENTERS

NO BIRTH CONTROL & NO SEX EDUCATION

NO HATING YOUR FELLOW MAN & NO JEWS IN THE COUNTRY CLUB

NO PORNOGRAPHY & NO END TO BEAUTY PAGEANTS

NO FEDERAL WASTE & NO CHECK ON MILITARY SPENDING

NO END TO WAR & NO DRAFTING THE WEALTHY

NO ABORTION & NO SUPPORT FOR UNWANTED CHILDREN

I live in the South (I travel enough not to be afflicted) and we have a saying, "You ain't a man 'til your daddy says you are and gives you a gun." I'm just as afraid of killer/robbers as the next guy and I do, in fact, have a gun at my house…but I don't have a survival gun, a commando knife, a machine gun, flare gun, .357 Magnum with armor piercing bullets, a silencer, M-16, riot gun with heavy duty buckshot, tear gas canister, or a stun gun. I'm just not that afraid.

On occasion, I have visited various "Gun 'n Knife" shows. I see guys walking around in jungle dress suits sporting side arms and reflective sun glasses. They walk as if they were stalking "commie cruds" right there in the air conditioned convention center. Their cold steel eyes and curled lips give the impression they are

soldiers of fortune on temporary leave from the Angola countryside or the jungles of South Africa, rather than Acme Office Supply or any number of middle class businesses that let men wear jeans and T-shirts while getting a little sun. What do these people think about? Getting hurt or bullied in front of their girlfriends is my guess. NO CALLING THE SHOTS!

Americans have this thing about "bearing arms." A goodly portion of them are mostly concerned about bearing arms to flea markets where they can sell them to other people who are afraid of life and want to bear arms. "You'll take away the Sportsman's right to hunt stuff!," we hear from the gun lobby (people who make money on guns). Sure, the M-16 and stun gun are great "sporting"devices…ask any deer. One reality of gunmanship is the fact that most guns are paid for with cash that Uncle Sam (a substantial gun guy in his own right) doesn't get to tax. Guns become valuable, untaxed inventory, like having a few bars of gold or a sack of diamonds around the house. Rather than using cash, you can trade guns or use them as collateral for loans and nobody is the wiser…like a great traveling garage sale, one can pack $100,000 in the station wagon. It's a business, not a sport!

The rub comes when some dumb dude gets mad at Bubba Earl over at the Hi-Ho Club because he has stolen the affection of Loretta Lorent and runs over to Charlie's Pack-a-Pawn and buys a $30 pistol made in Taiwan or some other Micky Mo country (where we get cheap labor) and returns to the bar just in time to plug

Bubba as he gets in the Muscle Truck. Some of these guys love carrying a pistol in their belt so the lump will show…like a rock star sticking a wadded up sock in his crotch. If you're a gun wimp, it becomes imperative that you let people know you have a gun. When they get bored with that, then it requires that one shows people he is willing to use it…man enough to use it. The rest is History. NO THINKING!

The important fact about a gun is you don't need to be within anyone's personal space to use it…you can be running and fire over your shoulder. The gun is the preference of cowards because it requires very little physical conditioning. Since most heroin and coke freaks are in poor shape, the pistol comes in handy. The only people lower than these people are the nose-bleeds that sell them the guns.

So what's the answer to this question? I say all guns should start at a hundred bucks and should require a 30-day waiting period, so records can be checked like a driver's license. If you have ever been arrested for anything bigger than a traffic ticket or back alimony, forget it! A crime with a gun should have a mandatory prison sentence that scares people. Or better yet, the real solution to the gun problem may be to stop worrying about guns and make bullets cost $50 each! NO SHOOTING PAINS. ★

146

In the late 1800's America suffered one of its first bouts with the nouveau-riche mentality when every "Jo Bob" in the country that made big money from the industrual revolution or the Civil War wanted visual proof of success. One of the most obvious images was that which came from marrying off one's daughter to a withering person of title in Europe. Young women, fresh from the better schools of cultural breeding, were encouraged to become Baronesses, Princesses, or at least "Ladies" on the arm of a European gentleman of position. In many cases that arm was propped up by the efforts of a doctor in attendance. Everything European was good and a sign of arrival for its possessor. These marriages were actually mergers with the poor girls as pawns, who have been irrevocably hindered in the art of survival outside of an artificial environment. NO FRENCH TICKLERS!

French wine, French fashions, Italian shoes, German cars, Swiss watches, Dutch chocolate, Irish linen (nothing comes from England except Lady Di fashion tips), Greek olives, Russian caviar...doesn't America make anything worth a flip? You bet we do! Let's get past this Europe worship. We'll buy anything that has a "La," or "Le" before it, or an "O" after it. If someone came out with trash bags called La Junke, Le Waste, or Trash-o, they'd sell a million, especially if they were overpriced. The problem with this country is that it's full of suckers who want to prove they've made their first $30,000, or that they have superior taste. NO TASTE!

You might be interested to know that gourmet shops in France offer a version of Campbell soup that's the same stuff we get at 7-11...only it's priced three times higher! That's right! European nouveau riches buy our products to impress their peers. A spiffy cocktail party, over there, might offer Cheetos or Fig Newtons washed down with a Slurpee or a Mountain Dew that had been smuggled back from the USA. Let's get real here. We don't need a bunch of biscuits from a foreign baker who's too tight on sugar. Folks, their cars are small because they don't have much steel; they don't have good tortillas because they don't have much corn. The English don't have good hamburgers because they have so few cows...in fact, they eat organs like kidneys, brains, and too much liver...stuff we throw away. German cooking specializes in rotten stuff or things that have been soaked in brine. They eat eel, which they catch with a dead horse's head on a string. The Dutch drink blood of cow and eat rotten cheese with green stuff all over it! Is this what we adore? NO ROT!

I say: Get past it!...when it comes to Europe Love. Let's start finding out what we have right here at home. Go to Yellowstone Park. Go to the Grand Canyon...the Empire State Building is taller than any tower in Europe. Who needs a tower that doesn't even stand up straight? NO LEANING ON EUROPE! ★

"The Baby Boom Calls the Shots." I feel this is the basis of current American society. The fringe groups are either too old or too young to have a feeling for that state of mind. Those older than 33-39 years are certainly wiser in many areas, but I'm not sure they really understand what NO means to the largest single group of people who ever lived in the history of the world. The competition level alone could never be understood by people whose heyday was in the 1930-40's. Granted, some things never change, like raising children, buying a house, pride in your country, and dealing with people. But some things do change, like the meaning of success in an inflated economy, rules for parents in a two-career family, pressure that says the end of the world is next Thursday, test tube babies, transplants, sex changes, and artificial insemination. In the past, an idea took about six years from concept to consumer... change was slow and everyone had time to adjust. A new idea can be conceived and on the shelf in six months now. Just as we get comfortable with one concept, we have five new ones. The "Information Boom" is terrifying because it doesn't produce anything but information: stacks of paper, columns of figures. Things you can't show your kid when he visits your office. If there IS a major NO sign that probably represents our time, it might be NO LOSING OUR GRIP.

During the fifties, the power structures that called the shots offered NO to just about everything we wanted: NO SILLINESS, NO ROCK & ROLL, NO PETTING BELOW THE BELT, NO DANCING TOO CLOSE, and, most of all NO QUESTIONING THOSE WHO SAY NO. The only time NO fell from favor was when you spoke of America or of the opportunities of the future (unless you were black). The word NO just didn't exist when it came to promises for happiness, success, and eternal bliss. We were filled with promises that parroted our elder's dreams... elders who swore we would never suffer the lives they led. We, the greatest generation in history, marched forward with shields painted bright red with words reading YES, YES, YES! It just didn't occur to most of us that the same message had been given to those before us. We didn't realize that the same giant NO that had leveled every generation before would be waiting to stop us like a giant catcher's mitt of reality with a little label sewn in the back that read: NO STAYING YOUNG AND INNOCENT. When some of us looked closely, we began to read the fine print, written by the same order that had caused our parents to place all their hopes in us... NO FAIR. It DIDN'T say NO CRIPPLES, NO ALCOHOLICS, NO DIVORCE, or NO TRAGEDY. The reality of life set in.

Even though it took a terrible toll on many of our generation, the NO word brought us to our senses. By seeing the negatives of life, rather than hiding in false hope and blind promises, we were able to assess the situation and make some decisions. Once we accepted the presence of all the NO's we began to appreciate any YES word when we found it, even if for a fleeting moment. There were some YES days with a few NO's and vice versa. We found that a NO usually didn't last long and the promise of a YES on the horizon was enough to raise our spirits. Without the fear of failure, we really couldn't enjoy the sweetness of success. For some poor souls, success came to mean the total absence of NO or negatives — a foolish, Utopian dream that can only lead to failure. Life is full of NO. It always has been and always will be. There were no "good old days," except when we were children. Trying to form our lives or those of our children in such a way as to deny reality is to practice folly. I say study the negatives in such a way that they can be dissected and dealt with. We can't destroy pornography, but we can teach our children that it is not so evil as it is boring. We can explain our bodily functions in a manner that is pleasing, rather than in a tone of disgust. We can speak of the love of our fellow man, rather than his conversion to our way of thinking.

Many of us are scrambling to produce artificial YES signs in hopes of drawing attention away from the big NO. Religion, career extrem-

ism, compulsive fitness programs, massive accumulation of riches, IRA's, and elaborate insurance programs might just be a futile way to overshadow the biggest NO sign of all times: NO GETTING OUT ALIVE, the one sign we should easily accept if we have any real belief in a natural order of things that would give us life in the first place.

The word NO is a big part of America. It gives us something to push on, push against. It's a sounding board that lets us know we are alive. I think we should take the NO (the negative) and find a way to live with it as we do rain storms, summer heat, and relatives with a bad laugh. Many would desire to spend their time only in that which is positive. They would say: "Why look at the bad? Try to see the good in everything." How nice. Unfortunately, it will be the negatives that bring us down. To say they don't exist or that they only exist for others is to live without experiencing true emotion, and in ignorance. Ignorance is capable of being overcome, but we don't know because we don't want to know. We have allowed our institutional doctrines to become so strong that the slightest crack of questioning NO will cause total collapse. No political, cultural, or theological dogma can be of true value unless it can withstand negative questioning or have the ability to laugh at itself. The silly question might be the first indication of positive growth. This can only come when somebody challenges the well-entrenched YES with a positive NO. Our sacred cows need to be checked for hoof and mouth disease if we are ever to know the true value of NO in America. ★

This is not a picture book, but rather one that gives us a certain picture of America, from California, across The Rockies and Great Plains, along the Atlantic and through New England. These photographs cover a time span of 25 years.

NO signs are everywhere. There's no escaping them. They lurk at us from walls, windows, doors, buildings, fences, trucks, roads, and even trees. They are at train stations, bus depots, and airports. Wherever we travel, a NO sign lingers about—in cold bold, striking red, in scrawled letters or fancy script. They are "signs of the times," an anthropological-sociological measure of America; they are words penned by pundits, poets, philosophers, and would-be comics.

But there's something more to their literal meaning than meets the eye. For embedded in the metal, wood, plastic, or cardboard message, there is a soul—a subtle hint of a personality who made the sign. In effect, these signs reflect human character.

I wonder who that person is behind the sign. I conjure up an image of an individual telling us *SORRY, NO FREE MATCHES.* He's a grouch; a rumpled-looking fellow always frowning. Whereas the creator of *NO DOGS, VICIOUS GARDENER* is an urbane, smiling Ivy Leaguer with a second home in the country.

I never did meet the person who made *NO DANCEING* (sic). I was a high school student in the '60s when I saw this sign. It made me aware of the existence of "No" in America.

I didn't take photographs back then. So I took the sign instead. I don't know why. The sign was hanging above an old juke box in a pizza shop.

How *NO DANCEING* remained in my possession for so long is amazing. It's really a fortuitous sign because it germinated the idea for this book five years ago when I rediscovered it in a carton of old papers.

Since then, I have photographed more than 300 NO signs in various parts of the country. They are an eclectic bunch: misspelled, graphically ugly, some barely readable with letters faded by the weather. Others are funny and cute. Some have drawings. A few are downtrodden. Most are upbeat.

I saw these signs inadvertently while walking or driving. Often I felt as though a magnet were pulling me into a situation or place where, to my surprise, a NO sign was hanging. For example, the time I made a wrong turn down a country road near Poughkeepsie, New York, and found *NO PERMANENT PLANTINGS* wired to a cemetary gate. Or the day I was in Ephrata,

Pennsylvania, and walked into a public restroom that warned in large letters *NO LOAFING*. Then there was the truck-stop cafe near Reno, Nevada, off Interstate 80, where a sign attached to the food cart told patrons *NO DOGGIE BAGS FOR BUFFET*.

I am basically a people photographer. I like to shoot subjects that move and human conditions that are moving. At the outset, this book posed a challenge. How to photograph words and make them visually exciting? While there was the slight technical problem of solving glare—many signs were behind glass doors or windows—there was also the problem of dealing with some unwilling people who wouldn't allow me to photograph their NO sign. How absurd it seemed! Here they displayed their sign in the open public, yet refused having it recorded on film. After a while, sensing who might be "paranoid," I didn't ask permission, and just shot the picture anyway, figuring that had I asked, I'd have been turned down.

In retail stores when I sensed this "being-refused-if-asked," I had a tactic. I bought something, then took my photographs while the clerk rang up the sale.

Generally though, people were cooperative and I didn't have to play games. They were friendly and amused about the book idea. Some even gave me leads for other NO signs nearby.

Most of these signs were shot with a wide-angle lens, either a 20mm, 28mm or a 35mm. Occasionally, I used a 55mm macro (close-up) or a 105mm telephoto. When possible, I juxtaposed the sign with candids of people. Also, I incorporated other elements into the frame to establish a point of reference and to make the photograph graphically interesting.

Though some of the signs are a conscious attempt to be humorous, most of them are just plain funny without trying to be. Nor is there any deeper, underlying message than what they already spell out.

This book is merely a collection of seriously-silly photographs in which I took delight in discovering a positive side of no. Cha, cha, cha.

Mark Chester

Mark Chester, San Francisco, 1986

During my vagabond years when I took these photographs, there were many who sheltered, fed, and supported me in one way or another so that I could get moving again, real fast. My grateful thanks to: David Butwin, Murray Candib, Philip Cecchittini, Paul Fagin, David and Pamela Glazer, Maurice Kanbar, Rik and Marilyn Karon, Joyce Konigsberg, Chong Lee, Nancy and Paula Lichter, Tom McAfee, Bill and Felicia Schwartz, Barry Solloway, Ron and Eileen Solomon, Ruthe Stein, Katherine Tillotson, Brenda Walker and others who extended my credit…and my stay.

Also, a special note of appreciation to editor Bobby Frese and his colleagues at Taylor Publishing whose enthusiasm guided this book to its publication; to Paul Hobson for his stylish design and good judgment; to George Toomer who tackled the text; and to Edwin Newman who graciously contributed to and supported this book from its inception.

All negatives were shot on Kodak Tri-X film. Photographs were printed on Kodak Polyfiber paper by Gamma Photographic Labs of San Francisco.

All photographs were taken in the United States, with the exception of those on pages 37, 128, and 148.